Nothing in Reserve

true stories, not war stories

by Jack Lewis

This is a work of fiction and nonfiction. Names and stories, fictional and factual, are rendered from the author's imagination. Any resemblance to actual persons or events is entirely coincidental. Truth is always a discovery, never a scheme.

Road Work and *Purple Hearted* originally appeared in *Operation Homecoming: Iraq, Afghanistan and the Home Front*, edited by Andrew Carroll, published by Random House, 2006.

Game Day originally appeared in somewhat altered form in *Soldier of Fortune Magazine*, published by Omega Group Ltd.

Published by Litsam, Inc.
Shoreline, WA, U.S.A., http://www.litsam.com

FOR MY FALLEN BROTHERS
—SGT Michael "Iron Mike" Pitzen, *back tattoo*

...and for my girls, of course.·

TABLE OF CONTENTS

AFTERWORD

because the words always come after, don't they?

My wife Melanie—Hu Mei Li, on her birth certificate, for those playing along in Mandarin—and I went down to Green Lake, where we used to run.

Back then she would assure me, in her slow Texas honey drawl, "You're the only person I could ever run with."

Then I couldn't run anymore. I could watch her, though, and I still liked that.

So I set myself onto the gravel path near the paved way, moving carefully along under the trees, mostly avoiding the open. She switched on her headphones and stepped out with a runner's strut.

I watched her prance away from me. It was getting close to the last time. I had a job now and Mel had offered to help me find an apartment. I had stopped asking questions after she requested that I pet-sit over Thanksgiving so she could holiday in Wyoming.

We didn't know anyone in Wyoming.

I stumbled around the lake for a while, wondering why I was there. The spangled boobs of proud runner girls didn't do much for me anymore, and if I stayed around people too long that right ear of mine would start pounding every time.

Still, I walked for awhile out near the public promenade. It was a warm, breezy day and the fireworks of Independence Day—the fireworks that had inspired me to wash down codeine pills with a liberal beer ration and to turn the TV up loud—were two weeks in my wake. My universe smiled, extending the prospect of a not-bad day.

Feeling a little obnoxious, I pulled out a cell phone and dialed my daughter. The little girl who dragged my buffalo plaid flannel shirt around as her special blanket until it was tattered to feathers had grown into a teenager more interested in hanging with her buds than jawing with her old man, an occasional presence with nothing new to teach.

"Sweetie? Hi."

"Uh, hi, Dad."

"Hey, I was just wondering if we could get together in a couple of weeks. I can get over to Walla Walla pretty early on Saturday…"

"Saturday is Fair day."

"Well, that's alright, id'n it? We could—"

"I have to see my friends."

"Oh."

"The weekend after is a family trip, and then I'm in school."

"Y'know, I'd like to see you once in awhile, Kiddo."

"Well, you've been pretty hard to get hold of yourself, Dad. And Mom has a problem with you when you don't take me on times you're supposed to have me—like last Christmas."

Touché.

"Well, do you think you could find some time? I'd really like to—"

"I'll see."

There was some background noise. I heard her stepfather call Malia's name.

"Dad, I have to go."

"Okay, sweetheart. I love—"

There was a click at the other end. I tucked my treacherous little phone away into a belly sack, and walked a ways further.

When my stride degraded, I went to the side of the trail to rest my knees and back. There was a bench there, facing northwest over the flashing blue lake. A bronze plaque dedicated this bench to Blanche Marie Duvivier, 1998, with the epigraph "life is a bowl of queries." In yellow paint across the fir planks, somebody had stenciled **GROUP W BENCH**.

So I sat there.

Arlo Guthrie, the original Group W conspirator, was an old hippie by then, but old hippies wear better than old soldiers. My wives and my daughter and my army were all done with me.

Lacking anything better to do, I sat down and started to write.

Your work is to discover your work, and then with all your heart to give yourself to it.

—Buddha

KICKIN' IT.

We get up in the black, down the coal town road;
And we hike along the track where the coal trains load;
And we make the ponies pull till they nearly break their backs
And they'll never see again down the coal town road.
—Allister MacGillivray, *Coal Town Road*

Twelve men dressed to kill slipped quietly through a twisted cobblestone alley, passing gate after gate until they moved up on their objective: a steel door, brush-painted in a primary color that would show up brightly at daybreak. Hens in a nearby yard muttered fitfully and shook out their feathers.

The lead scout said, "Hit it."

One soldier blasted the latch with a ghetto-grip 12-gauge shotgun, then two husky privates swung a black, steel ram through the gate. It clanged like Edgar Allen Poe's alarum bells.

Once, on a joint op with the Iraqi National Guard, the Iraqis heard the shotgun and promptly fired on the breaching team with their BKC machine gun. Happily, they were calmed into ceasing fire before they accidentally hit someone. Just as happily, they weren't with us this time.

"MOVE!," said the leader and our patrol poured through the gate, fanning around the walls, covering high and low. Nobody needed further direction. We'd all been here before, in a hundred different compounds that were all just the same. Green and red laser dots danced along the palisades, probing the villa. As family members stirred, Surefire weaponlight beams split the darkness of their rooms and bleached out their startled faces in hot, halogen white.

The family lined up docilely, and we separated the men from the boys to sit them cross-legged in the front courtyard. They, also, didn't need much direction anymore. Iraqis in our target houses usually didn't make a sound, even when they were armed as most were. Most people are uninterested in fighting to the death. Anyway, our targets were usually asleep when we arrived.

They weren't different from us because they "hated us for our freedom." They were different because they had no custom of privilege to fall back on when soldiers kicked in their door.

While the captain asked questions through his terp, the rest of us poked our muzzles into sugar sacks and efficiently ransacked every compartment of the house, unfolding blankets, pulling apart recycled snarls of grubby wire, pushing up ceiling tiles. Habitually, I trotted upstairs to look around the roof, checking over the side for "squirters," our term for suspects trying to exfiltrate through the cordon. If they were suspects, they'd run. If they ran, they were suspects.

QED.

My neighbors back home would have demanded a warrant, just like folks did on TV. If detained overseas, they'd querulously assert, "I'm an *American citizen!*"

This family had no such delusions of corporate influence. Even in their own home, they never imagined saying, "I'll have you know: I'm an Iraqi citizen!

"Now get out of my house before I sue you blind!"

Who would care a tinker's damn for their so-called rights? No one ever has. Not Saddam, not the sheikhs, not the Republican Guard, and not us. Surely not our critics back home, fervently asserting that our cure was worse than the disease even as they advocated consigning a few more billions to the fiduciary oversight of Kofi Annan's number one son.

Peeled from their beds, our target family stood blinking outside in their sleepwear, silently hoping we wouldn't take their men. That decision would be made by a 28 year-old captain of the U.S. Cavalry, cavalry being a mish-mashed quasi-branch of the army's combat arms professions.

One older gentleman, with a long gray beard, was allowed to rejoin the women. His wife—why is it always an old lady?—decided it was time for some answers. She jabbered questions at us.

"Shut her *up!*"

The terp murmured quiet lies until she switched her tactics to resentful glances from her burning eyes.

I thought of our neighbor Alana back home, and her stouthearted, raging granny continuum of civil disobedience and loud resistance to both civil authority and corporate influence. I thought of Mom defiantly providing sanctuary to illegal refugees.

Why *is* it always an old lady?

Now that we'd breached noise and light discipline, may as well smoke. A couple of replacements looked around bewildered, like there was something they needed to do if only someone would tell them, but most of these soldiers had gone through a hundred doors at night.

This target was ranked as a low probability for harboring insurgents, but our squadron commander hated for his men to sit idle and squander his chance to be a blooded combat commander.

"The 'God of War'," Russ called LTC Pingel, "making enemies faster than we can kill 'em.

"What was our PSYOP objective here again?," he asked as we lit up another smoke outside.

"Something to put on the daily report," I answered. I smiled crookedly at Russ. "Keep your eyes peeled for PSYOP opportunities."

Two cav troopers joined our brief brotherhood of nicotine.

"Scariest thing I ever seen?," said the bigger of the two fresh additions to our smoking circle.

"Mm?"

"*Hajji* wouldn't come out the bedroom, so we bus' th' door in."

Boring.

"Yeah?"

"We caught 'em mid-fuck. Nothing but big, hairy, *hajji* ass bouncing all around in there. The hair was all on *her*, too. Nas'iest fuckin' thing I ever saw."

"Oh, that is *all* wrong."

"Hadda find me some seriously good porn after that," he said, pausing to drag thoughtfully on his smoke, "clear my fuckin' head out."

The harsh white lights poured over the courtyard walls while helos beat at the dry air overhead. It felt like an action-adventure movie set, on a night shoot in Los Angeles

No.

It felt much faker than that.

FRATRICIDE

And what is well and what is badly—need we ask Lysias, or any other poet or orator, who ever wrote or will write either a political or any other work, in metre or out of metre, poet or prose writer, to teach us this?

—Plato, *The Phaedrus*

It started with my dad calling my brother a criminal, and my brother calling my dad a crazy old man.

It started with three—count 'em, three—landslides of a critical slope area at our Eastlake building project that resulted in lawsuits from the general contractor, insurance carriers, engineers, neighbors, City of Seattle and even the new owners. Not to be outdone, my brother sued, too. The slump of our soil-nailed hillside during what I called the "double Noah" of 80-plus days of rainfall marked the collapse of family business, family ties and future prospects.

Our company had been going great guns. We had walked tall and talked loud and called each other "meat eaters" over Salads Nicoise at the Palomino Café.

"If you ain't the lead dog, the view never changes," my brother would chortle, reveling when some risk-averse banker's lack of business *cojones* and pure gut instinct opened yet another opportunity for the surging fortunes of our Lewis Companies. As Chief Operating Officer and all-purpose money guy, Pete knew about these things. Dad was the Chief Executive Officer.

My card said "Vice President," which I was pretty sure didn't translate as "lead dog," but we were going places in fast cars and corporate jets with our pretty women. I wore handmade shirts with French cuffs that I couldn't afford. My view changed every day—at least, our corporate vision did. Maybe I was playing a leading dog role, after all.

Grinding down a series of fancy pickups at the rate of 52,000 miles a year, I made a third less money than our head technician, but the trucks were tall and they drove shiny.

I was a non-custodial parent who barely saw my daughter, but I was building her a future.

I was tired all the time, but I lifted weights before dawn and ran lap after lap around Green Lake with Melanie.

Then it all fell in.

Progress became intangible, then illusory, then invisible. Lawsuits and counter-suits piled up. Pin-striped and jut-jawed, we argued our way through the conference rooms of half a dozen high-rise Seattle law firms, losing virtually every round.

There came a day when there was no further point in showing up. We'd just be left standing coffeeless in the foyer, looking out over Elliott Bay and waiting for a quick handshake from a paralegal too busy to admit us to the inner sanctum.

Slowly, painfully, we degenerated from malaise to corporate quagmire.

Our company stopped paying bills and servicing accounts, and TV screens went snowy around Lewis County. The deal we'd been working to take over a larger entity in partnership with a Texas broadband venture cratered, and my forward-looking business plan for rural cable modems over optical fiber was no longer worth the creamy archival cotton paper it was printed on.

My fancy GMC rolling office went back to the truck monger. Dad's new V12 BMW was peddled off in bankruptcy court. Pete went shields-up and moved out of state to tend to his hotel. I took a job as a floor clerk in a hardware store, and my erstwhile multimillionaire father became the plum-jacketed doorman of a First Hill condominium tower where he would hold the lobby door crisply open to admit his own former car dealer.

I dreamed army dreams, and I dreamed them often, but I never dreamed of combat.

My dreams were simple. They were always set at some post I had never seen. I was always late, couldn't find my unit, didn't know the chain of command, wasn't briefed on the mission, was out of uniform and dragging around a duffel bag filled with all the wrong gear. The kids around me were younger, savvy to a battle rhythm I couldn't make out. My shit was not together.

The dreams always ended with my unit forming up, and marching off without me.

It started when Melanie and I had just finished the Toys for Tots run, a mass gaggle that starts at Seattle Center and wanders around for five miles until you run through a gate in the cyclone fence and into the stadium, then stagger a further few dozen yards down a cinder track past bleachers holding several hundred other tired runners. Unless you're out with the frontrunners, that is, and there was no risk of that.

Still, I usually panted along at a pretty good clip for the first couple of miles, watching my wife's brown legs stepping along under her black ponytail and Nike cap, and envisioning the serious expression on her round, dark-eyed face. On a good day, I'd pass her once or twice. Most races over five miles, she'd wait for me at the end.

Officers run the army, and sergeants make the army run. Privates? They just run.

And run.

When I'd joined up at 19, it was the first time I'd ever run consistently for longer than a football season. I despised the long, lung-burning runs and only made it through by belting out the cadences and concentrating on the shame of falling out. Had it not been for the army, I never would have run further than from the front door to the mailbox.

Then I met Melanie, who was a runner born, and suddenly found myself pounding out five miles in the morning, down along the Elliott Bay waterfront where the grain elevator loomed out of the dark and looping back to my cracker box condo to squeeze out sit-ups and pushups before work. Seemed I would do about anything for that woman; in short order, I even married her. I hated running about as much as I loved my wife, or maybe it was the other way around, but the best part of running for me has always consisted in the stopping.

Chomping down a faceful of bagels and bananas after Toys for Tots, I stopped to squint into a freshly painted vehicle the event-sponsoring U.S. Marines had parked there.

"Hey, sweetie, come look at this."

"Yeah, that's great, dahlin'," Melanie said in her Texicasian drawl. "What is it?"

"It's a 'Humvee.' Stands for High Mobility Multipurpose Wheeled Vehicle."

"Terrific," she said. "Can we get back to the car now?"

"These were brand new when I was in. I never got to drive one. All we had was one-fifty-ones—they're like little jeeps—and old-style deuce-and-a-halfs.

"Stick-shift everything."

Two young lance corporals, who no doubt could have outrun me over a five-mile course wearing their Marine blues and towing trailers, made a manful effort not to roll their eyes at the sweat-soaked fossil eyeballing their tactical vehicle.

"Jack, I'm getting cold."

"Yeah, yeah, I'm coming."

Life beyond business had coalesced around garden nurseries and home improvement centers, vivid friends of whom we saw too little, and neighborhood projects.

One spring, we helped hammer together a play park. Later, Melanie and I wrote a grant proposal for the Cedar Park traffic-quieting initiative. I formed seasonal rhythms in the first place that had felt like home since basic training. I set up the sound system for our neighborhood's summer barbecue, hauled street signs for the block party along 37th and drove the company's old yellow bucket truck home to hang ice-blue Christmas lights along the high eaves of our yellow house when the good rain turned cold.

We had two cats in the yard, another three inside, and drawerfuls of expensive running togs. Melanie had cut her ties to Enron just in time and thrown in her lot with PACCAR, the Bellevue truck monger. I planted fruit trees, pruned them inexpertly, and harvested our penurious crop.

And then I woke up very fast one day to a strange sound, went downstairs and found my wife staring at the TV in the wee hours of the morning. Melanie hates TV news, and in those days she was not enamored of waking up before seven. I wondered what could have gotten her up, and to this day neither of us knows why she decided to flip on the news that morning.

"They flew a plane into the World Trade Center."

"Who? Huh?"

"Terrorists."

Like everybody else in the country, I grabbed for some kind of perspective. Like many of us, I missed—though I may have shot wider than most.

"Sure, sweetie," I said, trying to make my pre-coffee rasp sound soothing. "Somebody's reprising 'War of the Worlds.'"

She pointed at the tube.

"Just *look!*"

Without a further word, we sat on the edge of the sofa and watched the first great atrocity of our brave new millennium. We watched for a long time.

Then, in real time that felt slow-mo, the second plane hit.

What do you do, when you're a neighbor? What do you do for the neighbors you'll never meet when every gesture seems futile and most are?

We donated. Melanie and I waited five hours in line for the blood bank, sent checks to the American Red Cross, prayed our unchurched asses off and scribbled a note on handmade paper for the steps of the Shoreline mosque. It read, "You are still our Neighbors."

We looked, as everyone from Rudy Giuliani to the French prime minister looked, for what more we could do.

We had nothin'.

"Surely you don't believe anything this crook, this... this *idiot* says or does?," Alana asked earnestly.

"I mean, you can hardly call him the President."

A bubbling vat of whitish bovine parts held center stage in the garage of Javier and Maria, our next-door neighbors. Standing near a plywood-topped sawhorse table piled up with seriously authentic Mexican food including Maria's lethal *habanero* salsa, I sipped at a cold Corona and smiled ingenuously at Alana. I felt too mellow to be baited by our sweet old neighbor from across the street, who lived with her daughter in a house full of cats, antiques and tea cozies that was perennially plastered with a colorful plumage of protest signs.

It had been a pretty good day. Melanie had painted the plywood cat feeders I'd knocked up for her feral feeding stations while I cleaned gutters in the sun and pruned my little stand of fruit trees. The hard words we'd exchanged over whether or not I should reenlist into the Reserves or National Guard hadn't been forgotten, but were mostly subsumed into a honey-do truce.

I looked over to where Mel danced with innocent grace to a pumping salsa beat from the boom box in the corner. Surrounded by Javier's relatives and friends, each of them wrapped in thin cotton sun dresses and lace front shirts, she was getting her groove all the way on and smiling like she never did at home. I stared at my wife for half a chorus, dazed by the look I remembered from dating her, then looked back at Alana.

"Well, I don't think we should just do nothing, ya know?," I said. "My dad used to say, 'we're gonna do *something* now, even if it's wrong.'"

"And you thought this was good advice?," Alana asked. Her eyes were wide.

"Why?"

Somehow, it didn't seem fair to me that only one party to this conversation was drinking beer. Man of action that I was, the best answer I could think up was to smile indulgently and take another sip.

Alana wasn't finished winding her stem. After steaming for a moment, she said, "Sometimes, you know, I really *hate* soldiers.

"I just hate them."

I don't care what people say about Mexican beer. The sudden taste of piss and ashes in my mouth wasn't from the *cerveza*.

Alana was a wonderful, feisty woman with a conscience and a brain, but I could never comprehend citizens feeling morally superior to those who did their fighting for them—who performed what was indubitably the entire nation's dirty work—any better than they could understand killing fellow human beings in the name of the body politic. The neighbor lady and I experienced a temporary but complete breakdown of communication while we looked at each other as though we were peering through zoo bars.

"Y'know, Alana," I finally said, "I love soldiers."

"In God's name, why?"

"Because while we all agonize about whether they're doing the right thing, all they worry about is whether they've done enough.

"And we're the ones who sent them."

While she looked for an answer, another disembodied joint roiled to the top of the pot. It looked like a baby's leg.

"Well, you don't ever have to do that again," Alana finally assured me, patting my arm. "You've done your part."

Two weeks later, on a rainy afternoon, I left work early to drive to a federal in-processing station where I was weighed, tested, measured, fingered and contracted.

"I don't want to be married to an enlisted man!," Melanie yelled when she found out. A civilian fugitive from the Nicaraguan civil war and a corporate veteran of Enron, she was somewhat intolerant of introducing new variables. A Cold War veteran of Korea and a family company burnout, I was unimpressed by private sector stability.

"Well," I said, "guess you better find yourself an officer."

THIS IS MY RIFLE, THIS IS MY GUN

There's miners' little sons down the coal town road
Playin' with their cowboy guns where the coal trains load.
But they'd better make the best of their childhood while it runs;
There's a pick and shovel waitin' down the coal town road.

—Allister MacGillivray, *Coal Town Road*

Belly down in gritty North Carolina sand was as good a place as any to wonder what the Hell I thought I was doing.

Fifteen rounds I'd burned through achieving "battle sight zero," six more than I'd planned for, and I was way ready to get up out of there. I wanted to call my wife in Seattle, call my daughter in Walla Walla, eat a quick ugly dinner and then lie back on my rack to plow through a cheesy paperback while the kids went off-post for bad beers, bare boobs and fresh tats.

We'd lain prone for an hour. My knees felt every pebble, my elbows burned with grit and my back was torqued like a gymnast on a pommel horse. Maybe too old for this, a little, but who doesn't like to shoot?

Super-stacked thunderheads and the C17 cargo planes wheeling in and out of Pope Air Force Base clogged the sticky sky overhead. You could tell which aircrews were practicing. Those birds made steep, corkscrewing combat approaches, touched down briefly and then roared out at high angles of attack.

The serious flights, inbound from overseas with loads of redeploying and wounded soldiers, slipped down the standard glide path and kissed the runway like a lover.

You couldn't tell which of the clouds were serious, though. We were racing the thunder to zero and qualify before lightning drove us off the range. Nobody cared about soaking some soldiers, who are expected to be more or less waterproof, but barbequing the deploying Reservists with a bolt from the blue might have gotten somebody relieved for cause.

Our range safety contractors, old soldiers making their last buck from the military, thus preferred that any lightning strikes happen well off their facility. At least we weren't wearing steel helmets, which used to be downright scary under thunder bumpers unless you were already schizophrenic and jonesing for a hundred thousand therapeutic volts between your ears.

Our range wasn't closed yet, though. With a little help from the butt of my rifle and a few reminder twinges from the knees, I stood and opened my bolt for inspection, left-faced and range-walked to the qualification lanes to listen for instructions from the tower. Although the crackling PA system was hard to parse, the script hasn't changed in decades.

"Ready on the left. Ready on the right…

"Right side safety, hold up your paddle when you're ready. Hold up your paddle when you're ready. Hold up your paddle when you're—goddamn it, I said hold *up* your paddle!

"Ready on the right. Firing range is ready.

"Firers, watch... *your* lanes."

I missed the first target I ever aimed at on an army range, and it was the closest one.

On standard qualification courses, "Fast Freddie" jumps up just 50 meters downrange. If you were paying attention, you could hit him with a rock. But Fred's half-height silhouette pops up and dives back down quickly (thus the name), and I shot into the dirt berm trying to hit him as he ducked. Close only counts in horseshoes and hand grenades, goes the cliché, and rifles are a "point"—as distinct from "area"—weapon. So ol' Freddie survived his first encounter with PVT Lewis.

The rest of the vaguely humanoid outlines, from 50 to 300 meters, all pitched obligingly to the ground at the sharp cues issuing from my M16's muzzle. I shot as unconsciously as stroking a tennis ball; as running down stairs; as breathing.

I first joined the army in 1983, but I learned how to shoot at my daddy's knee.

When I was nine and my brother seven, we each received a Daisy air rifle for Christmas. Mine was a "105," which is the classic flat-stocked, lever action, funny-looking stick. 105s were low-velocity and had non-adjustable sights, but you could adapt.

It's important to adapt the gear you have.

My little brother somehow scored a fully stocked version with a rifled barrel and more velocity, which he promptly employed to pump a BB deep into the meat of my left thigh. Maybe Peter should have been the soldier in the family.

I toted that rifle around each weekend we had a visitation with Pop, but it still took a heck of a long time to go through the half-pint carton of BBs that sat next to it under the felt-skirted Christmas tree. Our daddy's orchard received no quarter during my lengthy practice sessions, and if the occasional ricochet stung my knee, I was undeterred. I just assumed my brother was in the vicinity.

From BB guns, we moved up to a scoped, .22 caliber, bolt-action Winchester. In what would prove to be my only juvenile negligent discharge, I perforated a Thermo-Pane picture window with it, fatally wounding a carved wooden seagull.

Is it any wonder the Boy Scout summer camp range bored me? They had .22s, but allowed only decorous, single-shot fire at paper targets on a 50-foot range. Every shot had to be individually approved by the range master. For a kid who'd shot hundreds of rounds and thousands of BBs, it was like a preview of being stuck in traffic. Or of United Nations rules of engagement for peacekeepers.

At age 14, I was given a .30-30 Winchester carbine, but by then I was already hunting with my granddad's .30-06 with a Leupold Vari-X 3-9 zoom scope mounted to it. In my high school years, that old rifle still shot dime groups at 100 yards. Come to think of it, it still does today.

In November of my first year after moving in with Dad for high school, the Sea-Mart Yardbirds store held its annual turkey shoot in downtown Olympia. My father offered a mild suggestion that he and I participate. By this, I intend to mean that he told me to get in the dag-gone car, get set to shoot and don't dag-gone miss under any dag-gone conditions.

When we arrived to stand in line, there were still a lot of frozen turkeys left to give away. Waiting there for our turns, we saw shooter after shooter walk away shaking his head.

The test consisted of drilling a moving red spot at the tip of a cardboard "turkey tail." The tail, riveted from its top and loose at the bottom, waggled as it rotated on a barbeque spit. You got two shots to hit the jerky, traveling dot, three-eighths of an inch in diameter and mounted on a brown background moving across a brown background.

"How they expect you to hit it with that damn cheap little gun?," muttered a guy in camouflage coveralls as he stalked away from the line. "I'm comin' back tomorrow."

"You'll nail it," my dad told me, patting my shoulder in the sort of vaguely familiar way that made both of us uncomfortable. "We're going home with two turkeys today.

"Lewis men don't miss."

So no pressure.

When I got to the front of the line, the attendant asked my father to step away. He looked at my glass brick spectacles, clucked sympathetically and handed me the very weapon most perfectly suited to indoor stalking of a pasteboard turkey butt: a Daisy 105.

Firing once from my steady sight picture, I ticked the roundel surrounding the little red bull's-eye just high and to the left. Applying modest Kentucky windage to the southeast, I tracked my cardboard quarry smoothly around its looping course, and gently squeezed off my last and second round.

Dad and I both took home free turkeys that year. The next year, only I did. The third year marked my third turkey, but that time I drove down to Sea-Mart alone.

Mobilizing at Fort Bragg in 2004, we had to qualify on each of our assigned weapons, not just our M16A2 rifles. That meant our commander 1LT Parrish got more paperwork, detachment sergeant SFC MacDougall got to stomp around waving his arms, my assistant team leader CPL Russ Bannock spent a day on the machine gun range, my driver SPC Will Mandeville got the day off and old-timer team leaders SGT Caruthers and I had to dust off our grenade launcher skills.

The M203 grenade launcher was slung under the barrel of an M16. It was an elegant package, so long as you weren't the guy toting it for a few miles. The last time I had fired one was in August, 1984 in the Republic of Korea, 20 years to the month before gunning our lanes at Bragg.

Back in 1983, blooping grenades with the Second Infantry Division in Korea was made more entertaining by the presence of dozens of vintage military hulks scattered around the range, both U.S. and Chinese. There was even a half-track out there, probably now worth real money to any collector bedazzled enough to tiptoe through a minefield of unexploded ordnance to get it.

Our battery commander made it interesting by allowing the two top qualifiers to let fly with M72 LAW antitank rounds, which were just plain, destructive, boy's toy fun. That was the only chance I ever got to fire a LAW. Like every one of us who fired on that range that day, LAWs are obsolete now.

It was another month in Korea's rice paddy stench before I got to qualify with my rifle. Somehow, during that time period I managed to engage in a brief altercation with a cavalry scout on Radar Site Seven, a facility we operated at the top of Soi San Mountain to keep tabs on the North Koreans.

If I'd realized he was about to sucker punch me, I might have taken off my specs or at least ducked. As it was, his fist crashed straight into my right eye—my shooting eye—with lens fragments from my improperly tempered Korean glasses leading the way. His knuckles ended up bloody. My eye made the site chief sit down and fan himself.

We had a ration truck due that day. Pressing a blackening t-shirt over my suppurating orb, I rode down the hill with the battery cook to have the shards irrigated out of my eye by a medic at Camp Stanley.

I had never been trained to shoot with both eyes open. I'd heard of it, but it seemed suspicious to me, like applying face cream or voting Democrat.

My eye bandage came off just in time for Echo TAB[1] to go to the rifle range, where I qualified at the Marksman level.

Marksman.

"Marksman" is the remedial class of military shooting, the shooter's short bus of shame. "Marksman" is a euphemism for just getting by.

Army weapons qualification is achieved at three descending levels: Expert, Sharpshooter, and Marksman. My father had shot Expert in the air force with a .45 Government Colt.

Military .45s are accurate the way square dancers are skinny: some are, most... not so much. But Dad had qualified Expert with his. Ask him; he'd tell ya.

Then, as he continued the tale, he went down to Texas and set the all-time record for air-to-air drone hits, launching Mighty Mouse missiles from the underslung drop pod of his F-86 fighter jet.

Great-granddad John Fax shot wolves and bears in the Yukon. My stepfather Paolo shot on the competitive rifle team of the Oregon National Guard for ten years and collected an atticful of shooting trophies.

Really, no pressure.

-----

[1] Target Acquisition Battery, a specialized unit marrying the lightning mobility of hard-wired field networks to the robust survivability of forward artillery observers.

I had recently qualified Expert with a grenade launcher on which I hadn't even been trained. I had qualified Expert with a battered Hydramatic rifle on my first go-round in Basic. I had qualified Expert with hand grenades, and with the sweet old M60 machine gun. I saw myself as an Expert.

An *Expert*, damn it!

One quick punch-up with a cav trooper, and suddenly I was an ex-Expert with a prismatic slit trench bisecting my dominant eye's view. The sight picture swam in front of me with a burn like chlorinated pool water. I was lucky not to bolo[2] completely.

When I DEROSed from Korea, I was assigned to the personnel security desk of corps artillery S2[3] at Fort Sill, Oklahoma. Surrounded by clerks and staff officers who cared only how well I could type clearance forms in triplicate, I quietly

---

[2] To bolo is to fail utterly. In my army, there were no partial failures; only complete successes... or bolos. No one ever said the word "bolo" quietly. It is a word custom-designed for top-volume shaming, and also rhymes nicely with "No-Go," meaning you will not advance to the next training station because, well, you boloed – e.g. "*BOLO*, trainee! You are a *NO-GO* at this station!"

[3] Traditional staff offices were S1 (Personnel), S2 (Intelligence), S3 (Operations) and S4 (Logistics, or "beans and bullets"). Later additions include S5 (Public Affairs and Civil Affairs) and S6 (Communications). In S2, we updated a lot of maps, and shredded several tons of classified material every month.

buried the shame of martial ineptitude to which I was relegated by corneal scarring.

Every time I crossed Lake Washington for a Bellevue eye appointment, my optometrist set her cool, white-enameled ophthalmoscope gently onto the bridge of my nose, peered through it and then exclaimed about the scar crossing the middle of my right eye, clucking over the shimmering glass fragments that remained shallowly buried in the corneal surface. My 2004 exam followed this pattern.

"Check the file, doc," I reminded her. "I've had that one for awhile now."

"Oh, right," Dr. Malik said, leafing through my records. She had hundreds of patients.

"Any trouble with it?"

"Not really."

"Ready for those bifocals?" She smiled her adorable dumpling smile.

"Not yet, please. We're deploying in a few weeks, and I don't want to have to re-learn how to shoot."

"Right. Well, when you get back, then."

"Good to have something to come home to," I told her, but it was hard to wink with that thing on my face.

At Fort Bragg, SGT Caruthers and I stayed after school on the grenade launcher range.

I'd fired Expert on this course, a legit one-miss tally that never mattered, anyway. Turned out no one was counting but me, but what the Hell. First time in two decades I'd shot the thing, and I could actually hit with it. This was becoming amusing.

I wanted to shoot more.

"Any day you get to shoot is a good day" is a cheerful enthusiasm shared by nearly all combat arms soldiers who have never been to war, and even a few who have.

The range contractors had brought plenty of rounds, but since not many team sergeants showed up to actually qualify on their assigned two-oh-threes, we had many rounds to burn after everyone present shot their lanes. It was faster and easier to shoot ammo than to turn it back in. There was much less bookkeeping involved, and the retired old soldiers running the show (who were about my age, thus nearly a decade younger than Caruthers) were uninterested in additional complexity. They encouraged any interested shooters to go ahead and git some boomage on.

Overhead, southern clouds grumbled black warnings of damp doom. Our Civil Affairs brethren rose as one, folded their lawn chairs, secured their Cheetos bags and trooped onto the bus.

Launch live grenades in a thunderstorm? Caruthers and I were delighted.

There's a terrible satisfaction in shooting area weapons. Rifles crack, kick a little, then drill a quarter-inch hole somewhere. Machine guns are better: they hop around animatedly, visibly chewing up any unlucky downrange target holders.

Grenade launchers? They're just giggly good fun. They go *POOMP*, kick like a shotgun and make either a chalk puff with practice rounds or that healthy, live-round "boom" we all cherished so dearly. Gratification doesn't come any more instant than that, so the two of us laid in the wet sand, popping every round they had to feed us. We burned off half a case of practice grenades before we got to the live babies.

On SGT Caruthers's second live round, the silly old fossil fired short into the dirt, 20 meters in front of our firing positions. Dirt pattered down onto our backs, my eardrums rang through the foam plugs, and we laughed like jackals.

"Yee *haw!*," went the gung-ho thinking.

Yee-fuckin'-haw.

"Private Lewis," my Basic Training company commander had asked years earlier, "are you standing in the correct formation?"

"I… I think so, sir."

"You fired Expert today?"

"Yes, sir…?"

"Did you miss any targets?"

"Yes, sir, I missed Fast Freddy, sir. Sorry, sir."

He peered at me oddly then. Immediately, I got nervous. A private's main job was to wonder what he'd done wrong lately.

"Stand easy, son."

Gently, the captain hoisted the thick-lensed, black-framed glasses fondly known as BCGs[4] off my nose, held them up and squinted through them. Both of our worlds instantly devolved into a Vaseline blur.

"Jumpin' *Jesus!*," he said. I knew what was coming next. I'd heard it a hundred times.

"These are making me seasick! How in the name of God did *you* qualify Expert?"

The captain poked a glasses temple into my eye as he put my specs back on, but I was standing at attention so I officially didn't notice. Then he pinned an Expert badge onto the left upper pocket flap of my BDUs, which came as a huge relief. For a moment there, I thought he was going to make me go back to the range and prove it.

No pressure.

But that long-ago captain, my first and most temporary commander, didn't have that in mind after all.

"More power to ya, Lewis," he said as he stepped back and we saluted each other.

"Drive on."

During Basic Training, all manner of commotion is made about shooting Expert or (better) "Eagle Eye" signifying a perfect 40 out of 40, but that hooah stuff doesn't necessarily take. Despite the 50 promotion points that an Expert badge carried, lots of soldiers didn't much care later on when they

---

[4] Birth Control Glasses. Black nylon frames, thick lenses, low-rent Buddy Holly look, traditionally accessorized with white surgical tape.

become mechanics or medics or clerks or cooks or artillerymen. But every soldier carries a weapon sometimes, and I was Hell-bent on knowing what to do when I picked up a battle rifle.

Second Platoon, Charlie Company started with 68 men and graduated 53. After getting our badges, the three of us who fired Expert were marched to the helipad for our reward: a half-hour ride with our feet on the skids of a UH-1 Huey "slick." First and last time I was ever flown in one of those old dogs. What a hoot! Like a scene from *Full Metal Jacket* or *Apocalypse Now*, I swore I could hear Doors music in the back of my head.

Like most of the equipment I trained on—M16A1 rifles and M60 machine guns, TacFire computers, hand-crank telephones and jeeps—Hueys were mostly gone from the army by the time I showed up again. But there I was, two decades later, trying to be useful and wondering whether my country really had called me to service or if it was just the voices in my head again.

Behind me, I dragged sparkling contrails of obsolescence. Maybe they were slug trails.

Standing in a foxhole at Fort Bragg in the steamy August of 2004, I wondered whether I'd even be able to discern dark green pop-up targets 300 meters away. It had been a bunch of years since I'd shot a rifle with iron sights, or even played a "first person shooter" video game. Taking a breath, I pulled my M16A2 softly against my shoulder and established a solid cheek weld with the stock as the tower bullhorn opened our range.

"*Firers*, watch... *your* lanes."

Fast Freddie popped up 50 meters out on my left, gave me the finger and I missed him clean as usual. Then I ran the next 39 targets like Minnesota Fats shooting Eight Ball for beers in a Milwaukee tavern. Apparently, I had adapted.

The next day, they took our rifles away.

"*Hoo*-yeah, baby!," CPL Conrad exulted.

Conrad posed shirtless with two of our brand-new M4 carbines, holding them out by their pistol grips in a Rambo pose while his new driver snapped digital pictures.

Larry Conrad was a big, sturdy bricklayer who had dabbled in semi-pro football and boxing. His dog tags indicated his religious preference as SITH. Conrad, who claimed to have been voted "Most Likely to Take Over the World" in high school, had sulked for days at the news we would not be receiving M4s.

The M4 carbine was originally procured as an ARSOF[5] weapon, and we were supposed to be a SOF unit. Civil Affairs

---

[5] Army Special Operations Forces included the famed "green berets" of Special Forces, Rangers, 160th SOAR (Special Operations Aviation Regiment, aka "Nightstalkers"), Civil Affairs, and Psychological Operations (PSYOP). Other units under USSOCOM (United States Special Operations Command) included the equally famed SEALs of the navy's SPECWARCOM; AFSOF (Air Force Special Operations Command, who ran Commando Solo missions for PSYOP support, combat controllers and para-rescue jumpers); and MARSOC (Marine

had theirs, but no dandy new rifles for us—with a first lieutenant for a detachment commander, we just didn't have enough pull.

All of us had been irritated when the top-heavy, officer-ridden Civil Affairs punks got them and we didn't. According to our reasoned, objective analysis, those pussies didn't even *like* to shoot. Now that the nifty little carbines, complete with combat optics, were bestowed upon us (thanks, taxpayers!), it appeared Conrad had completely recovered from his funk.

"I got *wood!*," he crowed. "Just *wait'll* you see what I can do with one of *these!*"

Conrad's father had been a weapons sergeant in the Special Forces, and that apparently left Larry with the obligation to disdain everything our little PSYOP detachment did as "weak." Conrad planned to attend Special Forces Assessment and Selection as soon as we re-deployed, and then to blow on out of our not-so-high-speed company. At times, Larry Conrad made it obvious that he was embarrassed to be seen around us, but at that moment he was in love.

With a rifle.

Because we were one carbine short, 1LT Parrish went without. But he made it clear that anyone who failed to qualify

---

Special Operations Command). In general, SOF units require higher levels of fitness and mental ability and are trained to a higher level than "big army" line units. Notable exceptions to this generalizing included FORSCOM's 82nd Airborne Division… and, some would say, PSYOP and Civil Affairs.

with their new weapon would have to trade him for his M16A2 long rifle.

Compared to the full-length "muskets," M4s do make a lot of things easier. Such as getting in and out of vehicles in a hurry, which would be important if our HMMWVs were burning like the ones we saw on CNN. Or quick handling in tight spaces, such as in the houses we knew we'd be breaching and entering, whether or not that was against command policy for PSYOP soldiers.

The M16A2 is a damned decent weapon, though, heavier and longer but appreciably more accurate than the shortie M4.

Also, I was going to miss my grenade launcher.

It's always nice to have options.

ZEROING AND TARGET ACQUISITION FOR AN M16A2

Continue to fire three-round shot groups and make corrections until you have a tight shot group in the circle on the silhouette.

(7) If your shot group is within the circle, your rifle is now "calibrated."

—Field Manual 3-22.9

Oddly, the more I yelled at SPC Mandeville to relax, the tenser he got.

Inhaling a few of the slow breaths I'd been advising him to take, I spoke gently for a change.

Our freshly issued M4s, brand new from the Colt works, turned out to be cake to shoot. From factory settings, mine had zeroed in nine rounds and confirmed with twelve. I only hit 37 out of 40 after that—barely Expert and my worst rifle qualification since the debacle in Korea two decades earlier—but it got me done and off the range so I could attend to getting my driver to shoot onto the paper. It was also the second-best score in our detachment.

Yeah, that felt important.

"Don't correct," I told him for the fourth time. "Make your sight picture the same every time."

"But, Sarn't—"

"Don't 'but Sergeant' me, son. You just want to shoot a small group. Don't matter where it is, long's it's on the paper."

"Okay, Sergeant."

"Now take a couple of breaths, then let out a little air and stop breathing just before you let go each round.

"Gentle, now."

SPC Will Mandeville had barely qualified Marksman with his M16A2 and had never even picked up an M4 before this day, but he stopped talking, breathed carefully and shot a quarter-sized group at 25 yards. When the crackle of fire died away and Range Control verified safety, I took a Sharpie downrange and connected the dots for him. With a final sight adjustment, Mandeville shot another acceptable group with his spiffy little carbine, finally surrounding the bull ring. I looked around, expecting we were the last of the zero range holdouts.

Four lanes over, CPL Conrad lay belly down in a mud puddle, steaming like a microwaved cat. He was still shooting for zero. The madder Conrad got, the harder he jerked the trigger. The more he jerked the trigger, the madder he got.

Mandeville grew a big pair of eyes. For him, this dream was too good to wake from. When Mandeville started out driving for SGT Caruthers's team, CPL Conrad had been his assistant team leader.

The big corporal had lorded it over him relentlessly. By the time Mandeville was assigned to me, he was beat-down like a junkyard dog: jumpy, flinching and ready to bite someone.

"Oh, my *Go—*"

"Don't say it," I insisted, grabbing him by the elbow. "C'mon, we're going to the tent.

"*Range* walk, Mandeville!"

Conrad never quite accomplished battle sight zero. Eventually, he stomped back to the tent, cussing his obviously deficient, factory-fresh rifle all the way. Mandeville, now properly zeroed and a little bit confident, qualified Marksman again. It was a high Marksman score, though. One hit short of Sharpshooter.

The only soldier to bolo out was CPL Conrad. He got his sergeant stripes the next day alongside CPL Flanders, my gunner Russ Bannock (who qualified Expert on both his weapons) and Big Danny, destroying by promotion the cohort briefly known as "Four Corporals of the Apocalypse."

SFC MacDougall's bid for master sergeant was rejected. Doog would have plenty of time while deployed to drown his bitterness in Kurdish liquor supplied by friendly Brit contractors, but at least 1LT Parrish finally got his captain's bars.

Caruthers and I each received staff sergeant rockers, giving us a little more juice to negotiate with supported commanders.

We were all dressed up with somewhere to go.

Yee-haw!

Months later, after all was said and done, SPC Will Mandeville would emerge as the most decorated soldier in our detachment. He would fell an insurgent from 800 meters with a miraculous, "golden BB" shot out of his stubby carbine. Later still, after recovering from wounds, he would attend Air Assault School in the same class with Conrad, and they both would go as buck sergeants.

Mandeville earned those Air Assault wings after we redeployed, but Conrad boloed that round, too. He gave up trying to qualify for Special Forces when he learned that failing out of any army school forever prevents admission to SF Assessment and Selection.

Like the grenade launcher range, however, qualifying on our new rifles didn't matter in the end. CPL Conrad didn't have to cough up his new rifle to the lieutenant. Nobody's records were updated after our second rifle range day.

Soldiers may come and soldiers may go, but the bureaucracy of armies is immortal and immutable. Even for something as vital to combat duty as demonstrable skill with our assigned weapons, we had mostly to complete the event, and to make it look good.

We thought we were shooting the bull, but we were just checking the block.

I never did answer the captain's question.

How did I manage to shoot Expert with that old, loose-bolted, oil-spraying, Hydramatic-built M16A1 from the training company arms room—me with my watery blue eyes behind coke bottle lenses? Same way I would later qualify Expert with grenade launchers, machine guns and pretty much everything issued to soldiers so we could throw fire at the enemy.

There's nothing *per se* wrong with the army's training technique, encapsulated in the acronym BRASS: "Breathe, Relax, Aim, Sight, Squeeze."

BRASS just doesn't go far enough. In shooting, as in the disciplines of weightlifting or yoga, competence demands careful, correct breathing. But skilled respiration only gets you out of the way of yourself. It doesn't motivate you. It doesn't complete the event.

At a single-digit age, I learned my secret to successful shooting. My trick worked like a talisman to bring home Sea Mart turkeys and later, veritable carloads of feathers and fur. My little trick even got me through a few firefights, because it's really very simple. Any fool can do it.

Scan your lane. Find your target. Softly tell yourself, "Kill it.

"Kill it."

MOVIN' OUT

I survived myself; my death and burial were locked up in my chest. I looked around me tranquilly and contentedly, like a quiet ghost with a clean conscience sitting inside the bars of a snug family vault.

Now then, thought I, unconsciously rolling up the sleeves of my frock, here goes for a cool, collected dive at death and destruction, and the devil take the hindmost.

—Herman Melville, *Moby Dick*

It was our turn to leave FOB Freedom.

SSG Caruthers's team had headed way out west of Mosul to support the First of the Fifth Infantry Battalion at FOB Sykes. Big Danny's team was split among two battalions in Mosul with his team sergeant stooging around the "D," screwing terps. Our commander's unalterable rule about not splitting the teams hadn't lasted a week.

My team had been re-inventorying our gear, fettling Elsa the Wonderhummer with extra first aid gear and sandbag flooring, and getting antsy. As a slice element, tactical PSYOP teams showed up out of the blue and almost literally sang for our supper. We'd have one chance to make a good enough first impression on our supported commander to allow us to run missions instead of pulling endless rotations of gate guard.

"I'm giving you to two-fourteen Cav," CPT Parrish finally told me, and my stomach dipped a little. Of course, we knew we'd be going out to a battalion-size element at some point, and I knew I'd have to polish up my rusticated social graces before performing my tap in front of an unknown colonel, but there's a clean, clear difference between knowing your job and facing that first day at school.

"Cool, sir," I said, faking a little imperturbable composure. "My guys're ready to go. Where's 2-14 at, and what are they like?"

"They're at FOB Marez, right in that same area where we rolled for Block Party II.

"Their colonel's a hard charger, takes no bullshit. He only wants to know what you can do for him."

"So he'll be mighty happy when I tell him we're professional bullshitters, huh?"

"Don't give me lip, Lewis. Just go meet with Colonel Pingel, show 'im what you got, tell 'im what you can do, and don't make any promises."

"Check, sir. Who's their Three?"[6]

---

[6] The S3 is the operations officer, responsible for mission planning. See note on staff officers, above.

"Major Bailey. He's a sharp guy. I think you'll get along with him."

"Call sign?"

"Rattlesnake. Look out for their XO,"[7] my commander added. "Major Crownbury's tougher than hell, but he broke his neck in college and he's been pissed off ever since. You'll recognize him right away. He has, uh... 'strange' posture and a big zipper scar up the back of his neck.

"The colonel's very old school," Parrish added. "He's got a RSTA[8] squadron, but he doesn't believe in hanging back and looking things over.

"He believes the cavalry should be out front, leading the charge."

"John Wayne in a yellow scarf?"

"Colonel Pingel likes contact, the more the better."

"Well, sir," I said, "that should keep us from getting bored."

After coming through a complex ambush with 2-14's predecessors, 1-14 Cavalry, I actually looked forward to the prospect of more combat.

God, I was such an idiot.

Not young—I didn't have that excuse—just an unforgivably callow FNG[9]. Thought we would make a

---

[7] Executive Officer. The "executive vice president" of a military unit, first in succession to command.

[8] Reconnaissance, Surveillance & Target Acquisition. Pronounced "rista," means keeping an eye on the enemy.

difference, could make a difference, as long as I kept the faith. Such a cherry I was.

Our lieutenant, a month or two away from his captain's bars, smacked me on the shoulder.

"Go. Get outta here. Do big PSYOP.

"Their command element will be here for a brigade targeting meeting tonight. Link up is at 2230, on the hill by the bombed-out palace."

"Across from the Mayor's Cell?"

"Yup, that's the place."

As I headed out the door, he yelled, "Don't forget to send in your daily reports."

"You betcha, sir."

Pulling up to their column that night, we parked behind the S3's Stryker. Cav scouts and officers hung out on the lowered ramp, muttered and smoked, function-checked the onboard electronics. Next to the looming shadows of the cavalry Strykers, Elsa the Wonderhummer looked like a beagle among bears.

I extricated myself from my VC seat—a dusty little kneehole surrounded by radios, FBCB2, PLUGR, microphone and map case—and introduced myself to the squadron's S3.

MAJ Bailey went about six-three and sported a Clark Gable mustache to further decorate his Southern gentleman

---

[9] Fucking New Guy.

accent. I had an instant vision of him retiring as a colonel to sip mint juleps on a wide, white-columned veranda, surrounded by sweet honeysuckle, jasmine and lilacs. Standing in the superheated night air, formally attired in camouflaged armor, weapons and radios, I thought it would be a mean thing to begrudge the man an iced julep in his retirement—although he would have to abandon the singing sycophants of sweaty field labor to the army. You can't take it with you in these unromantic times.

Later, when I saw him in the daylight, I would see from his right sleeve that he had run around in the "100-hour War" of Operation Desert Storm Iraq as a tank commander with the 24th Infantry Division, of which I had been an artillery section sergeant just prior to separating on my first go-round with the army.

I viewed his compact war through the cathode ray obsolescence of the 19-inch, black and white Sony crammed into a wheel-less, 28-foot travel trailer in the rural college town of Pullman, Washington. Stumbling back and forth across our six by six-foot living room, crooning to the baby in each arm, I watched Charlie Battery's MLRS launchers—including my old track "Challenger"—ripple off hundreds of rounds at Saddam's Republican Guard.

A few years later, the 24th went right out of business: decommissioned, cased their colors, a whole Rapid Deployment Force mechanized infantry division struck from the rolls like a dishonorable private. They were replaced at Fort Stewart by the "Rock of the Marne" 3rd Infantry Division of thunder run fame. Major Bailey could hang the 24th's patch on his right shoulder forever, but I had nothing from the Victory Division. I had nothing from my long-decommissioned TAB unit in Ui Jeong-Bu.

I had nothing.

The major pointed at Elsa the Wonderhummer. Her wobbly trailer overflowed with team gear and ammo. With Will Mandeville on the steering wheel, Russ Bannock on the squad automatic weapon and me in the hot seat, our firepower more closely resembled a Boy Scout troop than a cavalry troop.

"You guys drive around in that thing?"

"It's how we roll, sir."

"You're nuts."

"Tha's off the hook, man," murmured an enormous soldier who loomed up out of the night. That was SSG Aldo Hotchkiss, a yellow-skinned giant who introduced himself as "Hajji" and cordially rattled all the bones in my forearm. Haj had the biggest paws I've ever seen on a human. You didn't so much shake his hand as take a ride on it.

"What's your freak, Hajji?"

He gave me their frequency and we exchanged call signs, which Major Bailey instantly kyboshed.

"No way, Sergeant Psy Ops. 'Spider Nine-One' does not git it. Your call sign is 'Psycho,' and you are 'Psycho Six.'"

"Uh… not an officer, Major."

"Are you the command element of our psychological operations team?"

"Guess so, sir."

"Well, there ya go, Psycho Six."

If you laugh silently in the dark, no one can see you. I never had liked our tinky-winkie call sign, but SFC "Doog" MacDougall had dreamed it up and was determined to see that we held to it faithfully wherever we traveled in Iraq. He also wanted everyone to think he had jedi mind tricks up his sleeve.

Doog was a putz, I was a cranky old fart, and we were running with the cav now.

"You got it, sir," I said. "'Psycho' it is."

"Good," he said. "You brief the Boss tomorrow."

Sometimes at FOB Marez, before we had much to do, I would lie in my hooch and stare up at the ceiling in the dark, listening to the booms of mortars. Sometimes it felt like being paralyzed, or stuck in one of those "running through Jell-O" dreams, and I wondered whether I could even get up, even move when I had to.

Numbly, I wondered whether it would matter much one way or the other. But every time they dropped close enough, I felt the same galvanic energy surge that jolted me off my rack and out to duty every morning. I forgot my withdrawal, charged outside and herded my guys into a bunker.

They were my job and my trust, and I didn't have to wonder whether they were worth it. Missions and men are the simple, irreducible moral imperatives of war.

You didn't want to do that until the rounds blew pretty close, though. Too many false alarms and the team stops listening. It was a combat zone. Risk was normality.

Calculating the sound only worked when insurgents walked them in. If that first round was a ring-ding winner, then sorry, Charlie and lucky you—your shit was in the wind. So when we first got to Marez and I lay on my rack, I would imagine what that last boom would sound like, what it would feel like if it dropped right through the thin steel of my designer Italian cargo container.

My Army Knowledge Online profile still carried me as "Amber" for deployability because I had no DNA sample on file. I had no security clearance, either, but that was neither here nor there. Fungible soldier body, I deployed with a few quick injections and an interim clearance. I wondered, if Ali Baba's round fell in my lap, whether they'd find enough pieces to ID me without reassembling my teeth.

I wondered if I should get under the bed.

Our third night at Marez, Ali Baba walked a series of mortars straight toward our hoochal area. I yelled SPC Mandeville out of his hooch and chivvied him along into a bunker. SGT Bannock was already moving.

We covered our ears and huddled in our upside down culvert, trying not to whimper like a pile of abandoned puppies. But I had already lived to twice their age, and it was long past my turn to be protected. I remembered my promise to Will's dad, and squatted with my back to the open end of the bunker, ducking my head, covering my guys and hoping the guy would run out of ammo before he got to us.

He was dropping Soviet 105mm rounds. One-oh-fives had a 30-meter kill radius.

The third-to-the-last round landed six or seven meters behind me and sounded like the Fourth of July, cubed. Happily, it detonated on the top of the heavy steel "poo tank" and all the fragmentation sailed clean over our heads.

That round put half a dozen jagged holes in the door of my hooch and blew my window out, but I had pushed my wall locker up against the window on our first day there. Everybody laughed when I did that. My outlook was that FOB Marez probably cost a million bucks a day to run, maybe a million bucks an hour for all I knew, but it definitely didn't feature the kind of million-dollar views that called for a picture window.

There were two more booms before the salvo ended. We hung out in the bunker for a few more minutes in case the sumbitch was reloading and shared some smokes, tittering like kids skipping school. We'd learned a few days earlier, when our column was IEDed in Mosul, there's nothing like a near-miss to get your blood up. We hated bombs. We hated mortars. We weren't big on shooting at people.

The whole thing was oddly addictive, though.

"Well," I told them, bumming a cigarette from Russ because I didn't smoke, not really, "now you've been shot at, IEDed and mortared.

"You'c'n go home and tell people you got the full package."

We had been in the sandbox for two weeks.

"Holy-shit-that-was-loud!," SPC Mandeville said. He giggled some more, nervous and excited as relief drained away his adrenaline tide. In an hour, barring another attack or a sudden mission requirement, he'd be sluggish as a winter bear.

"I think," said SGT Bannock in his quiet, level voice, "I hate mortars worse than anything.

"Fuck mortars."

"Fuck mortars, fer sure!," Mandeville agreed.

There should be heroic pronouncements to make about the brotherhood of risk, about finding the best in yourself under the worst conditions; something about how freedom isn't free and it has a savor never tasted but by we few, we happy few and lusty men, standing tall against the skulking evil of Ali Baba. But we were hiding in a repurposed culvert, and they were just fucking mortars.

"Yeah," I said, lighting Russ up. One of our hands was shaking, and between us we burned his fingers but not that much. "Fuck a bunch o' mortars, anyway."

Will had his own lighter, a brushed stainless Zippo with the army's eagle on the side, and his own cigarettes, too.

I habitually stole smokes from Russ. He always seemed to have a Bic lighter in his pocket, and it was always dead, so I kept my own polished chrome Zippo full of fluid with a fresh flint. Damn thing'd make fire in a hurricane.

Owning a Zippo lighter is, like playing Spades in the guard shack, part of ambient army culture. The first time I made sergeant, decades earlier, I had bought myself a cool-guy camouflaged Zippo. It lasted for one field problem before I dropped it—for the first and last time—somewhere in the Georgia pine woods.

This time, I bought the shiny one. Before we left home, I went out in my shop and epoxied enameled unit crests onto it,

12th PSYOP Battalion on one side and PSYOP regimental on the other. Such totems are cheap, and indispensable in their way.

It wasn't until a few days later that we found out Ali Baba's last round hadn't landed in the road as we thought. It dropped straight through the plywood roof of a National Guard engineer unit's tactical operations center, wounding a couple of senior NCOs and blowing their computers all to hell. Three days from redeployment, and two guys had Purple Hearts fall on them out of a clear blue sky.

At least they wouldn't have to pack up their office equipment.

The next day, Russ and Will dove into another bunker when they got shelled walking back from the DFAC[10].

"You two are the Mortar Magnets," I told them. "You need to keep your distance."

"Hah-hah, Sar'nt Lewis."

"You think I'm kidding?"

Two days later, 2-14 got word they were moving Way Out West to pursue High Adventure at FOB Sykes, halfway between Mosul and Syria's southeastern border. CPT Parrish told me to remain on station and link up with 1/5 Infantry as they rotated back from Sykes. Then he told me to roll with 2-14. Then he told me to wait for further instructions.

_____

[10] Dining Facility, or what we used to call a "mess hall."

While waiting for further instructions, I wandered over to FOB Marez's mayor's cell and made "reservations" for two temporary hooches. These were a quarter-mile up the strip from the Rattlesnake command TOC, past their med tent and motor pools up by the semi-soft-shelled gymnasium.

We spent a quiet night there and got mortared the next morning before breakfast. Sitting in the row of bunkers in our underwear and PT shorts, holding our rifles close, we smoked and BSed for a few minutes, waiting to verify the all-clear.

"Didn't I tell you guys," I asked them, "to stay the hell away from me?"

I lit up another of Russ's smokes, and he passed me another one. "Fuckin' Mortar Magnets."

When they smiled that time it wasn't a nervous reflex anymore, but their smiles carried no mirth, instead recognizing the kind of knowledge that would never apply again, anywhere else in the world except in war—and all wars are the same that way. They had learned the smiles of men who would never again say goodbye, only "Godspeed" or "take care," "keep your head down" or "see you when I see you."

My boys had warrior smiles now, the kind of smiles that didn't wrinkle their eyes at all; that didn't stop them from looking out, even for an instant.

Since our command element was too busy sucking up to the brigade commander to figure out where they wanted to place their own teams, I went to talk it over with Rattlesnake's S-3, my putative boss. At their TOC, 2-14's commo sergeants and supply daddies were running around in the sweaty night, loading up, strapping down, making ready.

I felt a little guilty. Pre-packed, we were ready to go anywhere.

"What're you talkin' about, Sergeant Lewis?," asked MAJ Bailey when I put the question to him. "Course you're comin' with us. You're part of the cav family, now."

"Well, sir," I said, laying out all the options and possible courses of action the way I was trained, "TPT Twelve-Ninety-Two's out there now, and they have some knowledge of the populace by now, so—"

"I call bullshit on that, Sergeant Lewis," said the Three. It was close to midnight. He was banging away on his laptop, people were charging in and out of the busy TOC, and I had just confirmed that we would be lining up on the road at 0300. "Y'all are *cavalry* psy ops. Get used to it."

"Outstanding, sir. We'll have some fun."

Figuring that about covered it, I stood to attention and saluted, giving the old-time 24th Infantry salutation.

"Vict'ry, sir."

Glancing up, Major Bailey looked straight at me with a little question mark by his left eye. Twitching at a smile, he returned my salute.

"Goddamn right, 'Victory.'"

I faced about and headed for the door. Time to pack again, but we were already light on the ground. We'd probably get at least 90 minutes of sleep before our five-hour, alternate-route vehicle road march.

FOB Marez was blacked out as usual to prevent giving away too many targeting clues to drive-by mortar slingers. My guys were snoozing in the truck and I was sitting on the hood, tired but not drowsy, chilly but not cold, excited but not happy. I heard the armored door creak open like a vault, and Russ eased out into the night air to share a smoke. Up through the gunner's hatch drifted the lung-butter rattle of Will's stertorous snores. He sounded like a PSYOP deception mission to delude the enemy into looking for non-existent armored vehicles.

"My God, that kid snores loud."

"Yeah, I can't sleep in there. When are we going?"

"When they go. Supposed to be 0430, but that came and went 20 minutes ago."

Russ fidgeted. Having never been regular army, he cherished certain notions about military efficiency, mission effectiveness and punctuality. Hating to disillusion him, I silently resolved to let him tumble to it on his own: the army is a federal institution.

"When do you think we'll go?"

"Soon enough. FOB Sykes'll be there when we get there."

I lit up both his cigarettes, the one he was smoking and the one I was smoking. I'd bought each of my guys a couple of cartons of cigarettes, "so I won't feel guilty when I steal 'em," but I despised Will's cherished Newports and rarely filched them.

"I'll take the turret today."

Russ looked at me, I think. It was too dark to make out his face, but I saw his cherry flare before he spoke.

"That's okay, Sergeant," he said. "I've got it all set up the way I like it."

He didn't know I'd heard him fretting the day before to Will, about sitting up in the line of fire for five hours through Indian Country.

"No. You just had a go-round the other day with 1-14. It's not your turn right now. Besides, you have better ears for the radio.

"If we have a stop along the way, we can switch then."

"Alright, Sergeant."

About an hour after we left the wire, we hit the first big turnoff. I scanned the intersection as Will swung Elsa onto the two-lane, headed west. I was facing forward into the wind, leaning over Russ's 249 when I heard honking behind us.

Twisting around in the turret, I saw the XO of 2-14, MAJ Crownbury, waving us down. Dolled up in his very special, fringed buckskin cavalry boots, he was this day's convoy commander. I waved back, then hunched down into the turret.

"Mandeville, stop. *Stop!*

"Stop the damn truck!"

Smacking him on his helmet, I tried not to crash into the radio stack when Will finally heard me and piled on the HMMWV's brakes.

"Sergeant Bannock, did you hear a radio call?"

"No... ?"

From our clamshell truck, Russ couldn't see behind us, either. When the truck stopped, I popped back up. It was hard not to notice that we were now the tail end of the convoy. The big HETS behind us were nowhere in sight as the major pulled up alongside. I yelled down to him.

"What's up, sir?"

He finished jabbering into one radio net, acknowledged a call on the other, then yelled back up at me.

"You guys have a crew-served, right?"

"We've got a SAW." I was holding it loosely in one hand. A squad automatic weapon is not the world's most impressive standoff device.

"You've got a what?"

"A *SAW*, sir!" I held it up and shook it like a spear.

"Well, I need you to turn around and go back to pull security. The mechanics rolled the FRSH."[11]

"Rolled the *what?*"

"The *FRESH*, the—never mind. Can you get turned around?"

---

[11] Forward Repair System, Heavy. A large truck and heavy trailer carrying a very well-equipped, self-contained automotive shop. Pronounced "fresh."

"O' course, sir."

"I'll send somebody back here as soon as I can. You guys shouldn't be out here more than a couple of hours."

And his driver sped him on up the road, rapidly disappearing into the dust of the column ahead. It was suddenly very quiet. I couldn't see a U.S. vehicle in any direction.

"Mandeville, get this thing turned around right now."

"I'm on it, Sar'nt."

He started jacking the trailer around. I pulled our mike off its hang line and stepped all over the convoy freq, making sure they knew we were coming.

The FRSH lay on its side like a dog by the fire, smoking gently. Rounding the 90-degree bend at a speed slightly exceeding its spec, the FRSH'ss crew had obtained empirical evidence that maintenance trucks are not built for stunt driving. A stranded buck sergeant with an 82nd Airborne patch from his Afghanistan tour waved us down.

"Anybody hurt?," I asked him.

"Not too bad. Driver broke his arm. He's evac'd."

"Good deal. You running this perimeter?"

"I guess. Can you guard the road you just came down?"

"Sure."

I brandished the SAW again. It felt about as threatening as a Super Soaker.

"This is what we got. Couldn't stop a rumor, but what the Hell."

He stuck out his hands, palms up. We had three avenues of approach, with three vehicle-mounted weapons to overwatch them. A lone Stryker, bristling with weaponry, faced the northern approach on the main MSR, which was the closest a car could get to our *tête-à-tête*. An MP squad from FOB Marez's QRF monitored the southern approach with their HMMWV-mounted .50-caliber machine gun, leaving the western approach for us and our popgun.

"I'll be your dismount," the sergeant said, "over behind that berm. Can you overwatch me from the right?"

"No worries."

"Don't shoot me, Staff Sergeant."

He looked at our cut-down paratroop barrel with concern. I smiled down at him, said, "No worries.

"Haven't shot a friendly all week."

I don't think the XO lied to us. I prefer to think that he meant for us to get out of there in short order. MAJ Crownbury's character was never in question.

Due, no doubt, to malevolent fate, Crownbury wouldn't get those fringed boots dirty all year. He would instead master remote mission direction over the UAV feed, chewing me out for using too much toner in the TOC printer and cruising the FOB in a captured Lincoln SUV.

Crownbury would redeploy with gold spurs 'cause he was a *cow*-boy, *ba*-by!

I directed Will to a position where the truck was sunk into defilade but from which I could see the road, set a spare ammo box up next to the gun with its 100-round nutsack, and settled in to wait. Waiting, empty-minded but alert to pattern variations, was one soldiering skill I had long since relaxed into.

With the steerhammer sun pounding down on us, we sweated like extras in a spaghetti Western. And I looked and I saw under the sun that the race is not always to the swift nor the battle to the strong, neither yet bread to the wise nor yet riches to men of understanding nor yet favor to men of skill... and that Clint Eastwood was nowhere to be seen.

After a while, the FRSH caught fire. Chief Chekhov, the motor officer, ran up and put it out by draining a series of handheld fire extinguishers into the flames. When asked later why he risked his life for a truckload of tools, the chief answered, "Sir, my life wouldn't be worth living over here without those tools."

That act earned him the first of several medals. As a warrant rather than a commissioned officer, Chief Chekhov actually had to earn his. When it comes to medal quotas, rank hath its privileges. Why wouldn't it?

We enjoyed some air cover for awhile—two Kiowa Warriors with leftover fuel to burn after their primary mission— but they wished us the best and fluttered back north when their low-fuel warnings flashed on.

When the boom came from out on the highway, I thought the FRSH had blown up from some unseen internal fire. Happily, it was just another suicide car bomber out on the main MSR. Failing his final exam, he overshot our babysitting Stryker by about 150 meters before he hit the go-button. I hope his spirit rose above the wreckage, only to see us laughing out loud at his compound stupidity while the last flaming bits of car and bomber rained down gently over the desiccated landscape.

Rest in pieces.

We sat there for a long string of dusty, tired hours.

Russ took his turn in the turret, then Will, and me again.

Between times, we picked at MREs and pogie bait[12], forced down blood-warm Gatorade and recorded pictures on Melanie's digital camera. On my computer at home, transferred from a CD-R that was burned way off across an ocean or two, lurks an image of Will striking a jaunty pose behind Russ's squad automatic weapon and chicken plate. There's also the only favor Russ ever asked of me: a picture of him looking westward into

---

[12] Person Other than Grunt, pronounced "pogue," was a lighter slur than REMF ("Rear Echelon Motherfucker") but still a derisive description for a non-hard soldier who loved his comforts. Pogie bait, or non-military snack food, was also referred to as "lickies and chewies." In the same spirit, sweaters, balaclavas and rainproofs were universally described as "snivel gear."

the early twilight, a lean silhouette with his arm stretched out to hold the flaming sun up in his very hand as weapon, trophy, prayer.

You would think it might get your blood up, that first time, but it was really a lot like range training. The difference was only in the mental re-checking and wondering if the weapon would work as advertised. Wondering if it would jam, and whether I would be stricken with buck fever and forget to take off the safety.

Absent certain actions happening in rigorous order and with extraordinary rapidity, things could become rather urgent, rather quickly—and I had never actually qualified with a SAW. With the squad automatic weapon, Mark 19 automatic grenade launcher and .50-caliber machine gun, I'd had familiarization (or "fam-fire") only.

Earlier that evening, about three miles out to the west, I had been watching a bevy of compact white pickups gathered around a farmhouse. We had received an advisory about groups of white Toyota pickups being used by the Anti-Iraqi Forces. Apparently a number of them had been stolen or otherwise acquired for use by insurgents, and it bugged me that they were so close, but since I couldn't seem to make anybody take interest, I just squinted at them from time to time to make sure they stayed put. It wasn't as though we had any spare bodies or vehicles to send over there, and white pickups were common enough.

The little beige car came down my road at about 35 mph. I wasn't overly concerned by it at first. It was the fourth or fifth car in the past hour to get close enough for my dismount to step out from cover and put up his hand. Each had stopped, made an obedient three-point turn and motored back up the way it came.

This driver came steadily on through the darkling dusk. I hoped he would soon see the sergeant who stood in the road first gesturing at him, then waving both arms, then aiming his carbine.

Just in case, I laid across Elsa's roof, snuggling the SAW softly into my shoulder like a hunting rifle. The driver would wake up and slam on his brakes any second now. I knew that. But he was getting way too close to my dismount.

I thumbed the safety off.

The little car didn't slow down.

Kill it.

Out of the corner of my glasses, I saw my dismount raise his M4. Trusting in Russ's zero, I set the M249 sights on the front bumper just ahead of the radiator grill, tracked and squeezed and let Hajji push his engine compartment straight into my five-round burst, realizing that I hadn't really expected to shoot as I suddenly wished for the ear plugs I had never inserted. But the SAW is a sweet-shooting weapon, low recoil and relatively accurate, and I felt my whole burst punch straight into the engine.

Will and Russ flopped belly-down in the dirt and the orange ball screamed down in flames over the edge of the world. The car slewed to a stop in a sudden boil of white tire smoke.

I kept my head down on the sights and my gun on the car as our dismount trotted warily up to the driver side window, yelling and gesturing with his muzzle. A lean Iraqi in a gray *dish-dasha*[13] and red-checked *kaffiyeh*[14] waited as his car was searched.

In the gathering darkness, I function-checked our machine gun. Cordite smells the same all over the world.

Out on the highway, the Iraqis silently emerged to push their car backward up the road.

The dismount walked up to me afterward.

"Got a smoke?"

"Yeah." I reached down and Will handed me one without having to be asked. Leaning over the side, I handed it to the young-old sergeant along with my lighter.

"Thanks." He dragged on it for awhile, looking into the last orange tatters of daylight, then handed my lighter back up.

"It was a family."

"I saw."

"Two kids in the back, mama in the front."

"Anybody hurt?"

"No, but ya gotta be careful, Staff Sergeant. One round went through the windshield, right next to mama's head."

I breathed, smoked, exhaled.

"They were gettin' pretty close to ya."

"I know." He puffed for a moment. "I shot at 'em, too."

---

[13] Long, lightweight, loose robe worn by Arab males. A "man dress" in GI parlance.

14 Arabic head scarf, traditionally secured by a cord.

"How many holes in the hood?"

"Five."

"Well," I said.

The man had been standing alone on the road with a car speeding toward him on an unknown errand, two hours after a suicide attack. I took another deep breath, let it out slowly and bent my face into a half-smile.

"I'll be more careful, big sarge."

He looked up at me and held his cigarette straight up, like a tiny torch of freedom.

"Thanks."

JACKASS, THE MISSION

Concerning the difference between man and the jackass: some observers hold that there isn't any. But this wrongs the jackass.

—Samuel Langhorne Clemens, *Mark Twain's Notebook*

Cool winds reminded us that the sun was only thinking about coming up. Two chickens in a walled-off yard grumbled irascibly to each other. A couple of blocks down the street, our ride idled watchfully, waiting to return to base. Our ride was a Stryker armored vehicle belonging to Blackjack Troop.

Across the street, Will's can of spray adhesive produced a tiny *ssshht! ssshht!* sound as he mounted posters on one of the tall steel utility poles left over from the time when Tall Afar had a functioning infrastructure. Russ and I, in back-to-back overwatch, sniggered under our breath.

"Do you think he sees it?"

"He has no idea."

"He-he-heh. He's gonna fuckin' shit."

Will was completely into his work, as he should have been. After all, his faithful teammates were overwatching him with a carbine and a squad automatic weapon, backed up by the heavy machine gun on yonder Stryker. An implicitly trusting character, he had no worries. Further out than I'd let him off the leash up 'til then, Will mumbled quietly to himself as he worked. Meanwhile, his antagonist silently approached on velvet hooves.

"Here it comes!," whispered Russ.

"*Ssh!* Get back on your post." He moved back down the street to his assigned overwatch position. The threadbare donkey took another quiet step and stuck its quivering nose out toward Will. I raised my rifle and scoped the donkey.

It had an insurgent look.

Keeping his eyes on the pole—this was one concentrating kid—Will reached down to grab another wad of posters out of his assault pack.

"*Hee*-haw!"

Will made a rapid-fire double take, saw the donkey's snout a few inches away, threw his posters to the four winds and jumped, tripping backwards over a chunk of concrete and landing flat on his dignity.

The clearly feral donkey, curiosity now piqued beyond endurance, lowered its nose and advanced on its quarry. As it clip-clopped toward the prostrate PSYOP soldier, picking its way carefully through the rubble, Will crab-walked feverishly backward, dragging his rifle by its dummy cord.

"Hunh," I said under my breath. "City boy."

Will finally got up, dusted himself off, looked up and down the street and got his gear rearranged. Impatiently, he shooed the donkey back.

Ruminant curiosity, once inflamed, must be satisfied. As Will worked his way up the street, the donkey followed him every step of the way. Maybe it thought the spray glue was some kind of cologne.

Each time Will had his hands full with posters and glue, the donkey would nose-bump him, keeping it up until its face was pushed away. It seemed anxious to avoid rejection. For his part, Will was trying hard not to yell and wake the neighbors. You never knew if the neighbors were friendly. The safer assumption was always that they were not.

Will looked across the street with an urgent expression.

"Sergeant!," he stage-whispered to me. "It's sniffing me!"

Half a block up, Russ worked so hard to stifle his giggling that snot bubbled into his drive-on rag. Pretending to scan my sector of fire, I looked sternly over my shoulder at Will.

"Got those posters up yet?"

"The donkey is *sniffing* me!"

The donkey appeared to me to be female. With donkeys, it's not hard to tell.

"She must like you," I told him helpfully. "Get those things posted so we can get back on the truck."

Will shot another resentful look at Eeyore, shoved her snout away a final time, then picked up the spray glue and went back to work.

Ssshht. Ssshht. Will was just smoothing the wrinkles out of our program to encourage Iraqis to "Report Weapons of Mass Destruction" when the coquettish donkey grew tired of his rebuffs, got a little frisky and bit him on the ass.

"*Gaa-ah!*," he screeched, and there went the rest of our posters into the slurry of curbside sewage. Will charged the burro, wind-milling his arms and cussing like a drill corporal. Startled, it backed up three steps and looked at him out of one dark and rolling eye, a little alarmed but still clearly besotted.

"Sergeant!," Will squeaked. "This donkey's *dangerous!*"

Holding one arm across my face to keep the noise down, I laughed so hard that my nose bled onto my sleeve from where I'd picked out the crystallized street dust. Hardly showed on desert camo.

"Yeah," I said. "Pick up your gear and let's go."

But his yelling had awakened the dawn patrol, those local Turcomen devout enough to have finished their prayers and started in on breakfast preparations. Bearded heads appeared over ancient parapets. We gestured with our rifles for them to go inside until we left, but the Stryker crew was a little edgy that day.

BOOM!

Brick chips burst off the corner of a nearby building, ringing my ears like a cymbal crash. The .50-cal machine gun had let off a single round. Hot breath tickled my neck and I realized that Will had crossed the street, leapt the curb and manifested behind me so fast he must have got there before he left.

"What was that?!" So close he was practically packed in my assault ruck, there was enough white in Will's eyes to illuminate the pre-dawn street.

"Warning shot. People are moving on rooftops."

"Maybe we should get out of here, Sergeant."

I motioned Russ back down to the Stryker.

"Yeah, we're done."

"Hey, think y'oughtta pick up your gear?"

Will looked across the street, where his assault pack and supplies were disseminated in a perfectly radial pattern from where he'd been standing. It looked like his equipment had caught a direct hit from a mortar shell. Centered within this diaspora of propaganda tools stood a small, resolute, brown and white donkey.

She had the look of love.

LOBSTER TALES

By trying we can easily endure adversity. Another man's, I mean.

–Mark Twain

Back in the States, it was looking like a great night for a family celebration that was long overdue. At their condo overlooking the Sammamish Slough, Mel and I laughed at one of Dad's old stories while his wife finished dinner preparations. They had been waiting for us to show up for this welcome home feast, which I'd been ducking while I tried to remember how to act around civilians.

"C'mon in and sit down," said Isolde, Dad's long-suffering, iron-tough fifth wife. "Dinner's almost ready."

Nothing feels warmer, closer and more human than sharing food around a family table. Melanie brought her wine glass in. Dad and I set down our shot glasses of single malt. Everyone smiled, just a little red in the face, as Isolde brought in the steaming main dish.

"I hope you all are in the mood for—"

"You're gonna *love* this!," Dad interrupted her. He gets excited about food. It's a family trait. We may not be gourmands of training and refined palate, but we are perennially adventurous, enthusiastic gastronomes.

"Don't worry, sweetheart—*everybody's* in the mood for this treat," he said. "Ladies and gentleman, buoys and gulls, I give you…"

Dad swept the lid off the serving platter. The blood roared in my ears and I tried not to look at the *piéce de resistance* of the evening, a huge boiled insect hunched over the table:

"LOBSTER!"

Maybe we weren't pariahs, but we were a little odd.

Unpopular with the squadron command element and unattached to any particular troop, my team usually ate together whenever we could. On the Night of Roaring Puke, Will was at the castle with Apache One-Five, so Russ and I planned to eat supper chow together and lift weights at the gym later. It was our regular schedule on nights that we weren't on mission.

When I knocked on the door of the hooch he and Will shared, Russ looked out of sorts. He was pale and jittery and glitter-eyed.

"What're you nervous about?," I asked him. "We don't have a mission laid on."

"I don't feel right."

"Yeah, well, that smokin'll kill ya," I said, but he didn't laugh. Not even his usual sarcastic snort.

"I think I'm kinda sick." He looked at me sideways. "I puked a couple of times."

"Well, you sure look like shit on toast."

Russ was shivering, with his shoulders hunched and hands jammed into his DCU pockets.

"Need to see the medic?"

"Yeah, I think so," he said. "I was gonna come knock on your door and ask if I could go over there."

"Stand fast right here."

The medic tent was way to Hell and gone across the FOB. We walked over to that area to work out every night, but Russ was too ate up to walk a mile in his own moccasins just then.

"I'll grab the truck and drop you off on the way to chow."

When I roared up in Elsa the Wonderhummer five minutes later, Russ looked worse. All the way to the aid station, he sat in the shotgun seat hugging himself, breathing shallowly through his nose as he shook. The constant whiff of diesel common to all HMMWVs wasn't helping his stomach. Along the way, we stopped for a barf break or two.

"I swear, young sergeant, you kids today are too goddamn fragile."

Then I glanced over at him, and drove a little faster. He looked awful ragged.

After a pair of medics checked Russ out, the on-call doc wrote him a quick scrip for anti-diarrheals and some pills to settle his stomach. They told me Russ needed light duty for a couple of days. I refrained from telling them that we didn't have any light duty. Schlepping him back to the hoochal area, I parked Elsa and walked across the big field to chow.

Russ missed out that night. Sunday chow featured steak and lobster, front and center on the steam table. Now, the steaks KBR served out were fairly tough: gristly, greasy and over-spiced. Still, they were steaks.

Usually, the Aussie lobster tails were a pass for me. My stomach was strong enough to have competently absorbed various exotica from all over the world. I'd eaten heaps of Korean *kimchee*, fish eyes in Hawaii, chicken feet in China, South African croc stew, sheep testicles in Kurdistan and deer brains in Oregon—all without unpleasant side effects.

But like most guys, I stayed half-sick all the time I was deployed. We didn't yet know that KBR was serving us various improvisations on Dungwater Surprise.

Cracking those tails felt a little too much like tearing into the carapace of a big alien bug. Not to complain—our chow in Iraq tasted a damned sight better than I remembered from Korea—but lobster tails somehow didn't seem like a good fit for the desert.

That night was different. Having not eaten since the night before, I went whole hog on the weekend buffet line. I let them slap that big tail onto to my tray, where it sat there gleaming like a mossy stone from our drizzly beaches back home. Maybe it was to celebrate not being sick, or maybe it was because I had no workout partner and would skip the gym that night. Could just be that I'd missed lunch, that the food shipment was recent and fairly fresh thereby, or that my team had no morning mission and I could sleep in until zero-six.

One way or another, I was eating like a champion. I sat in that echoing tin barn with a rifle at my feet and vacuumed up an enormous green salad, bales of yellowish beans, the biggest lobster tail I could talk them out of and enough piled chunks of steak to stretch my rigger's belt precipitously. Scarfing chow like a starving private, I washed it all down with two half-pints of milk, three tall glasses of red Kool-Aid and a slice of chocolate pie with thin (but hot!) coffee.

I had one more task to perform before checking on Russ and hooching up for the night. With my little red light in hand to keep from being squashed by an FMTV[15] I walked across the FOB to our office, logged onto SIPRNET and fired off our daily report to the detachment back at FOB Freedom: ammo good, logistics taken care of, vehicle standing tall, one man out on mission, one man NMC – non mission capable.

And one man sitting in a bunker at a plywood desk, missing his wife again and typing up a report that no one would read, to the syncopated rhythms of scrabbling *Rodentia* and the dying air conditioner.

Two hours later, Russ scratched feebly on the door of my tin can. I woke up instantly to find myself wrapped tightly into my fart sack and shivering like a scared puppy. Stumbling to the door, I found Russ barely able to stand.

"Dude," I husked, "you look like shit."

---

[15] Oshkosh's "Family of Medium Tactical Vehicles" replaced the venerable "deuce and a half" 2.5-ton trucks as general-duty load haulers.

He sat there shivering, huddled under a fake fur blanket from the Hajji Mart.[16]

"I'm... pretty dehydrated," Russ said. I could barely hear him. "Can't stay out of the bathroom. Hey.

"You don't look so good, either."

"I'm okay," I said automatically, but I couldn't stop shivering. "We better get you back over to the medics, though.

"Hang on a sec—be right back."

That was my signature line over there.

"Be right back."

Seemed like I was always going back for one last, forgotten item; double-checking for mission changes; trying to do one more thing and holding my team from heading out until I got myself and our stuff squared away. "Be right back" was something I said even more often than, "I'm okay."

It occurred to me that I do this to my wife, as well. And to my daughter. I've done it to my parents, to customers, to friends, and to everyone I've ever worked with:

"I'll be right back."

Though I usually made it back eventually, I've never acknowledged the unearned forbearance they granted me by their patience and their grace. This was different, however—an emergent issue of practical immediacy.

---

[16] A series of small shops run by local people authorized to come on post. They traded in bootleg DVDs, cheap electronics, haircuts and tailoring in the modern camp follower idiom. No prostitutes on the FOB, though.

Careful speed-waddling, a weightlifter's grunting clench and determined management of a gurgling colon are skills necessary to an American service member's life in Iraq. It's much like scanning for IEDs in that failure to pay attention and react in an appropriate and timely manner frequently results in a highly inconvenient explosion. The unforgiving consequences of gastrointestinal mismanagement in the Middle East may shed light on the traditional Arabic fondness for bottomless apparel (but do nothing to explain the Mohammedan penchant for anal sex).

Skillfully coping with simultaneous outfall from both ends of the GI tract was another unpleasant challenge. Those were not the toilets you wanted to put your face over.

Our second trip to the medical tent turned out to be more challenging than the first. Hunched over the wheel and shaking badly, I couldn't hear Russ's warning croak over the rattling of my teeth. Weaving more or less down the middle of the taxiway at 15 mph, we almost took out three camouflaged Charger troopers hiking back to their hoochal area in the dark.

No wounded men bled onto the rolling litters of the aid station that night, either from battle or from the cattle guard on Elsa's nose. The medevac Blackhawks across the way spun up once while we were there, but didn't leave their pad and no Strykers rolled up with wounded.

Not that night.

The attending medical officer read a Centurion paperback while medics stuck big-bore needles in our arms and flowed a couple of Ringer bags into each of us, so fast that it liquid-cooled our cores and we had to be wrapped into scratchy, brown wool blankets. Dizzy is as dizzy does—when I laid down on the litter to get my IV, I almost rolled off onto the floor.

We were destined for a long night.

For the next several hours after returning to our pad, I rushed to my hooch door every few minutes to roar like a lion, painting the rocks outside in taxpayer-endowed surf 'n' turf. There was no way I could make it to the latrine in a timely manner. By then, it was raining hard enough to clear the putrid mess away. Northern Iraq gets its whole annual rainfall in about three weeks.

Every half-hour or less I ran for the stink box, puking on the way there, puking on the way back and puking into the toilets; trying not to puke into the sinks.

Gut liner ripped out so hard it felt like screaming and laughing and doing sit-ups all at once. Russ was worse off than I was. If it hadn't been for the juice bags they stuck in our arms, both of us would have been desiccated as sun-dried Pringles by morning. We asked for Immodium AD and were told it might kill us.

"You just gotta get it out of your system," our medic said. "It's the only way."

Not once during that night did I believe I would die, but I was certainly willing to consider it.

With the blinds drawn, it was still pitch dark in my steel hut when Will knocked tentatively on the door. I cracked it open, squinting and flinching from the sun like a B-movie vampire.

Will frowned at me.

"God, Sergeant, are you alright?"

"I'm okay." It was the only morning since we'd been in country that he had gotten me up, instead of the other way around. "How'd it go?"

"Oh, my mission went fine. Apache guys were all over…"

Mandeville delivered a 15-minute disquisition on his briefing that I tried real hard to track, but I was swaying back and forth and trying not to fall off the pallet I used for a stoop.

The menthol light in Will's mouth was nauseating me. My eyes itched. My knees and spine and elbows ached like a broken heart. Blinking, I wondered whether I had the fortitude to put on my glasses.

"Mandeville," I interrupted in a harsh whisper. My head was pounding.

"…cav guys came back, and they were all like—"

"*Mandeville!*," I yelled at the top of my croak.

He stopped and cocked his head curiously to one side like a big puppy. "Yes, Sar'nt?"

"You're going to need to go to the targeting meeting and the BUB[17] today."

That stopped him. "Me, Sar'nt?"

"You. I'm wiped out," I admitted. "Sergeant Bannock is worse off than I am."

---

[17] The Battle Update Briefing was a daily event wherein every staff office, subordinate commander and "slice" (teams or detachments like ours) briefed the SCO.

I was ashamed of myself for falling out, but there was no way I'd make it through the targeting meeting without vomiting all over an officer's boots.

"Well, um, what do you want me to, uh, tell 'em, Sergeant?"

"Show Colonel Pingel the products we developed for him, and the new ones from the D[18]. Give him our mission schedule for tomorrow, and let him know I'll be—hang on a sec."

I puked on the rocks again, a bitter, colorless bile that was all I had left to spray. My abdominal muscles felt like I'd been stepped on by a horse.

Will's nose wrinkled up.

"Damn!"

"Sorry.

"Okay, let him know I'll be in as soon as I can. Don't forget the daily report to Cap'm Parrish."

I gave him my computer passwords and laid out the protocol of targeting meetings. At the end of my mini-brief, I reminded him, "Colonel Pingel doesn't think too highly of PSYOP. Just give him the straight dope, sit down and wait for questions. He won't have any.

"He doesn't know what the fuck we do."

"Why do we even go to targeting meetings, anyway?"

---

[18] A tactical PSYOP detachment (TPD) consisted of three tactical PSYOP teams (TPTs) supported by a detachment called the "rear D."

"Same reason artillery does. Army calls us all downrange effects."

"Even CA?"

"Nah. They got their own gig in S5."

Mandeville put on an expression of deep concentration. "So, on the SITREP, you want me to tell our captain… that you guys are sick?"

I just looked at him.

"Roger, Sergeant. I'm on it."

"Thanks."

I backed into my cave and shut the door, leaning gently against it until it clicked. Usually it received a ballistic slam to ensure that the cheap Italian latch would snap in, but just then slamming it would have been entirely too painful.

Damned fragile kids, anyway.

Some number of hours later, soft metallic tapping woke me up again. SPC Mandeville was waiting outside, looking nervous and apologetic and pissed-off, all at once.

"What's up?"

"The colonel and all those officers totally took it out on me."

"C'mon in, man," I whispered hoarsely. "Siddown."

I pointed at the eight-dollar black nylon PX chair unfolded in one corner. Woozy, I sat on my rack next to a small jumble of Wooden Boat magazines, and listened to what had transpired at the targeting meeting.

Will still wasn't all that confident around superiors, especially after the ambitiously vigorous and regularly applied drubbings received at the hands of his first team. Still, he took his job seriously, worked hard and only stammered when he was pushed.

On our team, we pushed him all the time, but not just to wind him up. We wanted him to be able to deal with any situation, any time, and except for that one night behind the DFAC when he couldn't get his DCU buttons undone in time for an urgent piss, Russ and I thought he was coming along fine.

That all ripped open during the targeting session. The ops officer, MAJ Bailey, had teed Mandeville up for a long drive by the fussy little martinet who commanded Rattlesnake Squadron.

"They kept asking me questions too fast to answer, and then when I was trying to answer one question, they'd ask me a bunch more questions at the same time.

"Major Bailey asked me if I even *went* to PSYOP training," Will said, indignant and sad all at once, "and I said yeah, of course I did, and then the SCO asked me if I *passed* and they all laughed at me."

Oh, no, they *dit-n't*. To *my* troop? Unh-*uh*, girlfrien'.

My head was roaring, and I had sweated a pungent effluvium through my Under Armour t-shirt until it stuck to me like a wino's rain-soaked bottle sack. Obviously, it was time to brief the major.

"I'll handle this," I said, grinding my teeth.

"Sergeant, I don't know if you should go over there right now."

"Be damned if we're gonna be intimidated by these cav assholes."

"No, I mean… you don't look so good."

"I'm okay."

"Do you want me to—"

"I'm okay. You're released for the day. You did fine. Don't worry about anything."

Shaving in the latrine a few minutes later, I found myself staring back into the glittering eyes of a psychotic. Three days past a skull shave, my red scalp actually steamed. My face was corpse-white with fiery red fever points tipping the cheekbones.

Once more unto the breach, dear friends, but not before stepping into the box for another watery, brown salute.

I stomped into MAJ Bailey's office without pausing at the "Meeting In Progress" sign, and came to attention in front of his desk.

"At ease, Sergeant Lewis," he said. "What can we do for Psy Ops today?"

"Well, I can't do much for you, sir," I started, "if you're just gonna tear up my guy for shits and giggles.

"I mean, what the *fu*—"

"Whoa, whoa, hold on!," he said, waving his hands. MAJ Bailey's easy smile was gone. "We were just havin' a little fun with the boy."

"That what you call it?" I was trying not to weave too much, but the room was moving oddly. "That's bullshit, sir. That was a *bullshit* way to treat my soldier."

"I don't know what you heard..."

Bailey, four years my chronological junior but seven echelons and a commission above my single-rocker rank, smirked around the room, sharing the joke with the staff officers. Only Chief Horton, the gray-headed intel analyst, looked worried.

"Sergeant Lewis," the chief said, "we were just funnin' with—"

"Chief, I got this," MAJ Bailey cut him off, and CW3 Horton instantly turned to hunch over his targeting maps.

Deportment just wasn't an issue for me at that moment. It was a problem I had sometimes.

"Who the hell are you people to critique my team's PSYOP capabilities?," I said. "You've been circumventing brigade and MNCI[19] SOPs every goddamn week. If I didn't cover for you, you wouldn't get *shit* for product out here."

"I know."

"You want us to make your product on-site, totally against policy, and you won't loan us a terp or even let us print on your printers, and you've got the balls to tell *Mandeville* he doesn't know what he's *doing?*"

---

[19] Multi-National Command Iraq, the highest command element in-country.

"You're going over the line here, Sergeant Lewis," the major observed, correctly. We were, after all, there to support the squadron—no matter how hard they made it.

"Really, sir?," I said. "Well, lemme ask you something.

"Was one of you fine officers the honor grad at POOC[20]? If not, where do you get off criticizing what you haven't even taken the time to understand?"

If it hadn't been for the virus, I never would have popped my cork like that. That's my story, and I'm sticking to it. But my frustrations with squadron—in particular with their Squadron Commanding Officer, LTC Grady Pingel—had boiled to a head somewhere in my feverish brain. Now I was spouting blowback to a major I actually liked, despite his Rhett Butler affectations, when it was his boss that was giving me ulcers.

LTC Pingel's own people called him "God o' War" in laughing deference to his notion that he could exercise absolute control of his 17,000 km^2 sector by "dominating the battle space."

Pingel also despised PSYOP. His affection was entirely reciprocated, but we needed his network for little things like food and shelter, and Pingel didn't want to give up the status of having his own tactical PSYOP team. Vanity, thy name is co-dependency.

"There are two battalions in Mosul that don't have *any* PSYOP support, let alone a whole team," I blared heedlessly on,

---

[20] PSYOP Officers Course, the officer advanced course for psychological operations commanders. Pronounced "pook."

"meanwhile we're trying like Hell to support Two-Fourteen—I mean, Jesus, we built you a *radio station* with a pocketknife and a hammer—and you people're making it a goddamn uphill jelly push all the way."

"Sergeant Lewis," the major said ominously, "if you don't want to be here, I can put you on a chopper out of here tonight."

I'd heard that one before, every time the Cav command group's brainwave of the moment ran head-on into the published policies of brigade, the task force, MNCI or "echelons above God." And that was pretty often, since those guys were just as hardheaded as me. They figured any idea that occurred to a cavalry officer was, QED, a pretty damned good one. My "are you kidding?" looks hadn't made a dent.

"You firing me, sir? Because—"

"No, Sergeant Lewis, I'm not—"

"Because I'll pack the team up right now. We'll hook up with the next LOGPAC[21] and I'll be outta your hair for good.

"You're not choppering me out of here, though. My team and gear and vehicle go with *me*."

He looked at me. The smirk was gone, but so was the friendly crinkle around his eyes. The tone I heard next was colder than a Siberian hooker's eulogy.

"Are you quittin' on me, Psycho Six?"

I took a breath, and let a thought or two bubble to the top of my roiling head. Back at the ranch on FOB Freedom,

---

[21] "Logistics Package" was shorthand for a supply convoy.

Doog would like nothing better than to make a "training" point about how SSG Lewis failed to integrate with his supported unit.

And if we didn't have anything to do, even for a little while, we'd all be crawling the walls like camel spiders. The bastard had me and he knew it. TPT 1291 was a tactical team. Our purpose in life was to run operations with line units. It was never going to be much fun at Sykes, but at least we had a mission.

Lots of missions, actually.

"We don't quit, sir," I said, and let out a deep sigh. "You know me better than that."

He looked at me for a moment.

"Well, that's what I like to hear. Tell ya what, I'll make y'a deal.

"You get your rear D people to git off their fat asses and send you the product you been askin' 'em for, and I'll keep Colonel Pingel off your back, much as I can.

"He's just frustrated because he thinks we're getting the short 'n' stinky end of the stick out here."

"Hell, we are, sir," I started in. "But he's his own worst enemy and he's makin' it hard to help y—"

MAJ Bailey put his hand up, and I stopped. "It's his battle space, he's the boss, he c'n do what he wants.

"Do you and I have a deal?"

Then he stuck his hand across the desk. I went ahead and shook it. There wasn't a lot I could do as a staff sergeant, except my job. LTC Pingel had conceived his big hard-on about PSYOP a couple of years earlier when he got slapped down during the after-action review of a Warfighter exercise.

With the colonel's unabashed encouragement, his scouts had abused the rights of civilians and destroyed property all over Ft. Lewis practice ranges, and the squadron's attached PSYOP team called them on it. The graders weren't impressed by Pingel's snarling response that he wasn't going to "play softball with people who sit around, dreaming up ways to kill us."

The role players who got injured, most of them American civilians, were also somewhat less than impressed. Vocally so.

The colonel would never let go of that grudge. He also would never change his arrogant, "we won the war!" posture toward indigenous Iraqis. But all we could do was all we could do. Change the system from within, and all that blithering boo-hoo.

"Sure, sir," I said to MAJ Bailey. "I got no problem working with you."

Our handshake sealed a deal between men. I stepped back and saluted, acknowledging our respective positions within the hierarchy.

"Thank you, Sergeant Lewis. Now go git your sleep on.

"You certainly do look like highly polished shit."

I sighed again. "So I've been informed, sir."

"What's your next hard time?," he asked.

"Zero four with Blackjack, sir."

"You gonna be alright for movement?"

"Yeah," I said, trying to exfil with some dignity, "I'm okay."

On the way out, I weaved into the door frame of their bunker and staggered a little.

"Thanks a lot, sir," I wheezed, wobbling out into the hallway.

So that was the big day off for Russ and me. Other than R&R leaves, it was the only duty day we missed on a constant seven-day-a-week schedule for the entire tour.

That made us just like every other forward-deployed soldier. Someday, I hope to meet a civilian who knows the true meaning of "24-7." I'm pretty sure it has something to do with working a 31-hour shift, then getting shelled just as you start to fall asleep, then waking up two hours later to go start more mission prep in the dark, or climb into a guard tower.

What are you gonna do, anyway? There aren't a lot of entertainment options, and lying around just drives you crazy. You might as well run missions. You're going to be there all year, anyway.

We rested a little that night. Russ and I wolfed our butt-plug pills. We made our next hard time, and we made every hard time after that.

But I never ate lobster again.

ROAD WORK

*I want to have time to look for my children and see how
many I can find. Maybe I shall find them among the dead.*

—Chief Joseph (Nez Perce), *I Will Fight No More Forever*

"Six-seven's in the ditch!"

"Did they roll it?"

"No, they're up. I think they're disabled."

"Where's the colonel? Is the colonel's vehicle okay?"

The colonel's vehicle was okay.

I never heard the boom-*CRUNCH*, only imagined it
later, much as you'll have to imagine the rest of this if for some
reason you want to savor a little snack of horror.

There was strong braking, followed by a great deal of
shouting. Our Stryker armored vehicle (Rattlesnake Three-
Three, in this case) as always moaned through its monstrous air
brakes, ground its oversized diesel thoughtfully; its crew
compartment clattering and roaring and stinking of JP8 fuel,
akin to the engine room of a very large boat. There was bumping
and grinding. There was rolling and heaving and sweating.

And then it stopped.

The major said that we would need a combat lifesaver. I have that training. It wasn't combat. There were no lives left to save. But I dug out our CLS bag, because you never know, do you? And walked across a pitch dark highway. Somebody was wailing hypnotically, repetitiously, to an Arabic rhythm.

Darkness in Nineveh on a zero-illum night has well-bottom purity. Sans night vision goggles, every cliché applies—for instance, you can't see your hand in front of your face. You shuffle your feet forward, feeling your way, tentative as the blind. But there was a single car headlight burning, beamed back at the road like an accusing finger. When tactical spotlights suddenly hit the little car, we found the source of the wailing.

He was what I might have once called an old man. He wore a silver beard, a monumental, red-veined nose and a big, thick wool overcoat. He was hopping like a dervish, bowing rapidly from the waist and throwing his arms to the sky, then to his knees, over and over again in a kind of break-dance of grief. Next to most of a car.

His coat was a dark brown tweed. Herringbone pattern.

Down the road a hundred meters or so, Six-Seven's vehicle commander and air guards had dismounted and were standing around their vehicle in the ditch. Nobody had started smoking yet.

I walked to the car with the Air Force staff sergeant serving as our JTAC, and moved the older man aside as gently as possible. He was built like a blacksmith, powerful through the neck and shoulders.

It's hard to describe the contents of the car. They had been a young man, not much earlier that night. A cop or a fireman or a soldier would have simply said, "It's a mess in there." I used to be a fireman. I'm a soldier now. It was as bad a mess as I've seen.

I'm not a medic. We didn't have one with us. It's still my responsibility to preserve life. So I squeezed into the crumpled passenger area, sat in the crumbled glass, and tried to take the pulse from his passenger side arm (nothing) and his neck (nothing). I thought about CPR, but only for a moment. His driver side arm was traumatically amputated, and that side of his head was flattened. He was going cold in the night air, and what liquid ingredients he had within him, those that hadn't congealed, were slumping and dribbling toward earth to mix with the liquids seeping from his twisted, torn little car, still gamely probing its one remaining headlight beam into the night as if to prevent the next accident.

Up on the highway, GIs walked around, gave and took orders. By the car, our victim's father still capered madly, throwing his arms around, crying out to God or anyone. I asked him, in my own language, to come with me, to calm down, to let me help him. I put my arm around him. Our JTAC helped me guide the old Arab to the road. We sat him on the cold ramp of our Stryker.

SSGT Rivera, USAF, took my weapon safely into the vehicle, and I tried to assess the old man's injuries. It seemed impossible that he could be only as superficially scratched up as he appeared. Their car had been hit head-on at maybe 130 mph closing speed, and food-processed through the undercarriage of an eight-wheeled, double-armored RV.[22] His son's body was only loosely contiguous, but this man was whole.

---

[22] Reconnaissance Vehicle, the flavor of Stryker armored vehicle most popular with the cavalry. I can neither confirm nor deny that its LRAS3 could generate a detailed infrared view of someone dropping their pants two kilometers off, at night, inside a plastic outhouse.

His hand was injured, bruised or worse, and he had a cut on his left ear. Blood and brain matter was spattered over his front like Hollywood effects. I wrapped a head bandage onto him and tied it gently in back. It looked like a traditional headdress with a missing top. Every few seconds he would get animated, and I would put my hand firmly on his shoulder. He would not hold still long enough for me to splint his arm, but he let me gently wash his face with sanitary wipes. His breath was corrosive.

A cavalry scout wandered up, sucking on a Marlboro Light.

"Can't he shut up?"

"You ever lose your kid?"

This is a pointless question to ask a kid, of course.

We moved him into the Stryker, assuring him that no, we weren't arresting him. But he didn't care about being detained. Whenever he started to calm down, he would look toward the car and break into wails. I sat next to him, put my arm around his shoulder, tried to keep him from jumping around enough to hurt himself or a soldier. I held him tightly with my right arm. By the next morning, my throwing arm would be on fire. This wasn't the first time that tendon had been inflamed.

The quick reaction force brought a medic with them, about 40 minutes later.

"What's his status, Sergeant?"

"He has a cut on his left earlobe. I think his hand is broken." *I think his heart is broken.*

"Roger. OK, Sergeant Lewis, I got this."

"Thanks." *Bless you for what you do every day, doc.*

I got out of the way and let the medic get to work, letting the old guy go for the first time in maybe an hour. He started wailing again almost immediately. While the medic worked on him, the colonel's interpreter came over and fired a few questions at the man. It sounded like an interrogation.

They had been on their way back to Sinjar. The younger man had taken his non-driving father shopping. There were no weapons in the car—either piece of it. There was no AIF propaganda, nor were there false IDs. Had we stopped these people at a traffic control point we would have thanked them and sent them on their way.

The young man had been a student. Engineering. With honors. Pride of the family. What we like to think of as Iraq's future. His father now repeated his earlier, rhythmic wails in a soft undertone, staring blankly into the night. Sometimes, he would look straight into my eyes and say it louder, insistently commanding.

Finally, I had to ask, "What does he keep saying?"

The tough Y'zedi terp looked at me, disgusted, resigned, or maybe just plain tired.

"He says to kill him now."

The SCO strode over and ordered the medic to sedate the man with morphine.

"No, sir," the medic calmly disobeyed. "Morphine is for pain.

"Physical pain."

"Well, can't you give him something to calm him down? I mean, this is unacceptable."

"On it, sir," the medic said. He hadn't interrupted his work.

I walked away and lit a Gauloise. My ATL walked up, smoking. I didn't say anything. After a few moments in the black quiet, SGT Bannock said softly, "It wasn't anyone's fault.

"It was just an accident."

"I know." Inhale. Cherry glow. Long exhale. "Why we gotta drive in blackout—here—I don't get.

"If Six-Seven had turned on their lights a couple of seconds earlier…"

"Yeah. I know." And Russ went to help carry the young man's remains into the sudden lightshow of ambulances and police jeeps, surrounded by young Arabic men with steely eyes.

"Hajji," the super-sized staff sergeant who gunned the truck we'd been riding, stomped down the road to kick a little ass and get 67's recovery progress back on track. SSG Hotchkiss was due to retire soon, had a job lined up in Florida. He wore First Cav's huge combat patch on his right shoulder, one of the few men big enough to wear one without looking ridiculous. This was his second trip to war, and he didn't need this.

None of us do, I guess.

Within a few minutes, they hooked it up. It would be two weeks before that Stryker rolled outside the wire again, this in an environment where trucks totaled by IEDs were welded back together and sent back into harm's way in mere hours.

I went and sat on the chilly steel ramp of the major's Stryker. The cold crept into me. The old man sat next to me, quiet; perhaps too tired to continue his tirade against cruel Fate, careless Americans, war and its accidents.

We aren't the same, that old man and I—not the same at all. We don't share a language, clothing, cuisine or common cause. The most recent cultural touchstone we share may be the Old Testament. And I never saw my son crushed flat by a streaking steer hammer of whistling steel, never had my scion's brain flecks dabbed off my coat by an armed stranger speaking in tongues.

I haven't lost a full-grown son, only a tiny daughter. A baby. And she wasn't torn from me in a terror of rending steel, stamped out by a sudden monster in the night. Three and a half months old, Flavia slipped away like a soft exhalation, so quietly that her passing never woke her mother, twelve feet away.

I was at school that day, filling out an elective credit by making bad ceramics. I like to think our daughter kissed her mother on her way out, on her way home. I like to think, perhaps, she forgave us.

But still, sitting on the steel tail of the monster that killed his son, a father next to a father old enough to be my father, I knew. I knew exactly.

Exactly how he felt.

"Just kill me now."

We sat and looked straight into the lights.

PURPLE HEARTED

Greater love hath no man than this, that a man lay down his life for his friends.

–John 15:13

He was young enough to be my son. Annoying enough, too.

When I beat on his hooch door that morning to get him up for a mission, he was his typical floppy-jointed, addle-headed, eye-rolling self. It was pouring down rain, I was standing out in it wearing PT shorts and a raincoat, and I had no patience: "Git up, time to move.

"You're goin' down with Apache."

Long groan—but he'd known what the mission was since last night.

"Quit your bitchin', Mandeville," I told him. "You're lucky as Hell.

"You get to hang out at the castle, and I have to go ride the hatch in this shit."

Mandeville was going downtown to broadcast over the LRAD—i.e. "Long Range Acoustical Device," an ear-bleeding gizmo originally designed to warn boaters away from the exclusion zone surrounding naval vessels—while I was planning to charge around town in one of Charger Troop's Stryker armored vehicles, broadcasting pro-election messages, pre-recorded in Arabic, from a man-portable loudspeaker system.

"Yeah... I guess," he said, squinting and rubbing the back of his head, sullen as a teenager—which, at 21, he practically was.

"Be at the office no later than zero-seven-thirty," I told him, before throwing on a uniform and four hundred bucks worth of raingear to go there myself.

I was closing in on a peak experience of blood pressure when he slouched through the bunker door at 0729.

"I took the trailer off."

"Oh," I said. "How we doin' on fuel?"

"I filled it last night."

"Alright, let's get your pack together."

"I already got it, Sergeant," he said, pouring himself a cup of coffee. "It's ready to go."

"Damn, Mandeville. I hardly know you!"

Goofy grin from him: "I do what I can, Sar'nt."

And so I dropped him down at Apache's hangar, ran to the DFAC to score him a box of breakfast and presently, off he went into Tall 'Afar.

But I never made it out on my mission that day. After I assembled my briefing memo on new PSYOP products for the squadron commander and walked it over to the TOC, I ran straight into the battle captain.

He said, "Oh.

"It's good you're here. Mandeville's your guy, right? We got a report he was shot in the neck—"

"What?"

"…but apparently he was wounded in the hand. A fragment hit him in the chin, and it bled all over, and they thought he had a neck wound."

"IDF or SAF?" [23]

"We don't know yet."

"Are they bringing him in now?"

"We don't know yet."

"What's his condition?"

"We don't know yet."

"ETA?"

He looked at me. "We. Don't. Know. Yet."

Everything takes too long, and the cavalry's axiom is true: the first report is always WRONG. And so I grabbed my troop data notes to pass along Will's next of kin and blood type data. While I dropped off my product memo, the ever-kinetic CPT Murphy walked beside me, settling his casualty report on the move.

Then I dropped by Charger Troop to beg off my day mission and beelined for the aid station to wait on my troopie.

Everything takes too long, and Murphy's Law (no relation) never fails us: Mandeville couldn't be evacked immediately due to continuing contact, which required Apache's available combat power to stay on-site and fight. Apache's company commander rolled his personal Stryker out to the castle to pick up my soldier, but then they rolled over an IED on the return trip, engaging a complex ambush with automatic fire while Will sat inside, quietly bleeding.

---

[23] Indirect Fire, i.e. mortars (likely) or artillery (not so likely). SAF (pronounced "saff") is Small Arms Fire, i.e. rifle or machine gun rounds.

Everything takes too long. A disorganized gaggle of civilian fuel tankers had roads plugged up all over the FOB and it took twenty (20!) minutes for Apache Six-Six to move from the front gate to the aid station. Bureaucracy is everywhere; logistics govern every transaction of our lives.

When Alpha Six-Six finally rolled into the aid station lot and dropped ramp, my kid soldier was sitting inside, holding up a bloody bulb of gauze the size of his head. He looked mighty uncomfortable.

The first words out of his mouth were, "I'm alright, Sergeant."

Seems Mandeville had been making big, noisy PSYOP with his handy, dandy LRAD when the castle came under fire, as it usually did when that bullet magnet was in operation. He put down his DVR/MP3[24], picked up his rifle, and took up a security position along the battlements.

Yes, battlements. It was a castle, after all.

When the sniper found him, the neck-aimed bullet hit him in his forward hand, ricocheted off the lower receiver of his rifle, then dug into his armored vest with a heavyweight punch. A fragment of the bullet jacket flew up and cut his chin to the bone.

Faces bleed a lot. They thought he was all done, but the infantry and commo soldiers jumped to instantly and administered buddy aid.

I talked to them all later. They said Will wheezed pretty hard. They said he stayed alert and responsive.

---

[24] Digital Voice Recorder. Invaluable little tool for PSYOP and a good reason to mooch lots of batteries from the Air Force, who always had them and were good to us. Our DVR, neither issued nor authorized, came mail order (you're welcome, taxpayers).

They said he never complained.

What Mandeville did do, after he was shot: he quickly trained up a commo sergeant on how to run the LRAD so that while he waited for evac, he could continue his mission. He secured, or caused to be secured, all of his sensitive items and PSYOP equipment. He marveled at the bullet they dug out of his vest. He told everybody not to worry about him, joked around a bit and reminded them to keep their heads down.

Everything takes too long. At the aid station, one x-ray salvo wasn't enough; they had to go two rounds with that. The shaky-handed lab tech who tried to start Mandeville's IV failed five times on his right arm before someone else took it away and plugged it in properly, upstream of his bullet-raddled left paw.

Through all that, nothing but some wincing and the occasional, "Oww."

And this comment: "I'll tell you one thing. These elections better work. They better get democracy, and freedom, and their rights, and hot chicks in tight jeans.

"I hope I didn't take this bullet for nothing."

And so, although everything seemed like it was happening in slow-mo, SPC Will Mandeville was treated, given a bit of morphine, and presently evac'd to the 67th Combat Support Hospital in a Blackhawk helo.

I made sure he had his body armor with the souvenir slug in one pocket, helmet, coat and the bloody DCU blouse with his name on it.

They can wash it out at the hospital, I thought, but of course they burned it.

I held onto his weapon, which had caught the bullet after it exited through the meat of Mandeville's left thumb. That weapon was NMC and irreparable—it wouldn't ever cycle again without the bottom half of it being replaced. Later, I would have to strip rounds out one by one through the ejection port, and crush the magazine with Leatherman pliers before I could remove it. I prayed my driver's left hand would recover better than his rifle.

Then I stood and watched him lift off and fly away, and saluted him in my way. I doubt he noticed. He was trying not to drop his IV bag, which sounds like a simple trick until you try doing it with your one good hand while juiced to the gills on morphine and battling the shaky shock of adrenaline withdrawal.

I'd miss Mandeville out there, and not just for the work he did, which was plenty if I rode him hard enough. I'd miss him pulling dumb stunts, working so hard at not working that it exhausted him just to think about it, starting to do pushups just because I gave him a hard look, teaching me how to play Yahtzee (then beating the crap out of me), and schooling me at ping-pong on a trip back to FOB Marez until he got impatient and started whacking the ball too hard to spin it down onto the table.

Mandeville was a near-total dingbat with no sense of planning who still managed to get things done; a lazy sloth who worked like a sled dog. He was a good kid with bad manners; a high school tennis champion constantly tripping over his own size twelves. This was the overgrown boy I had to kick out of the rack every morning, remind him to check the oil, bring his gloves on mission, and shower periodically.

Mostly, he was just too much of a goofy kid for me to have expected him to take it like a man.

Mandeville never wanted to deploy to Iraq. He wasn't some graying retread vet chasing faded notions of duty, honor and country. Will wanted to chase women around Seattle, go to college and find out what he wanted to be. He wanted to play video games, drink beer and buy a Mustang.

Guys my age were supposed to gripe about how "kids today" were letting the world go to Hell in a hand basket, how there weren't any standards for behavior anymore—after all, *we'd* taken such good care of the place. It wasn't like we were passing along a turd and expecting them to polish it… right?

Maybe it was because guys my age usually worked with guys my age. Guys Mandeville's age were just parts for the big machine in civilian life: laborers, clerks, apprentices. Mandeville went straight from busboy to combat soldier. Now WIA, he didn't even have the good sense to snivel about it.

After he finished flirting with the nursing staff at 67th CSH, he was flown out for further surgery at Landstuhl, Germany. As they loaded him onto a C17 bound for Europe, Will fretted only about letting down my team and our detachment.

I don't ever want to hear any more whinging over the passing of "The Greatest Generation." Ain't never been a generation better than his.

SPC Mandeville didn't take it like a man. He took it like his brothers across the generations, and earned his flagon of mead at Valhalla or at least his schooner of Bud at the local VFW post.

He took it like a soldier.

GAME DAY

Democracy is the theory that the common people know what they want, and deserve to get it good and hard.

—H.L. Mencken, *A Little Book in C Major*

It's a wonder I wasn't shot in the head.

Two days before the election, I was sitting on top of a school in Tall 'Afar, screaming at the top of my batteries. My manpack loudspeaker was shoved up against the wall at the edge of the roof. It repeatedly squawked out the eight pro-election messages I had pre-recorded on a borrowed MP3 player, plus a couple of messages Charger's terp had recorded that morning to give credit to the passel of commandos who were officially securing the poll site. Charger Troop, 2-14 CAV Rattlesnake Squadron, with its several Strykers, three machine gun positions and attached infantry squad from Apache CO, was officially just backup.

I didn't really see why I needed to be down there 24/7. There was no night-time mission for PSYOP to scream at civilians in the dark. But what the hell; whatever gets you out of the office, right? The annoying bit being that, since Russ was detached off to Task Force Tacoma and Will had inconveniently gotten himself shot, I had all the team equipment to hump around, solo.

C'est la guerre.

Previously, I had dropped off election banners to all the troops, plus No Parking and No Roll[25] banners. Charger Troop managed to get one No-Roll banner up, next to a hospital entrance where drivers had no access anyway. No other banners were posted anywhere in town, and Charger Six didn't want to give back his banners for me to post.

He wanted souvenirs.

Charger had recently gotten itself a new commanding officer. CPT Halsey, who had moved over from S4 when he got promoted, was doing OK as far as I could tell. Besides, it was hard to begrudge a few souvenirs to the guy who called me "the hardest working man on FOB Sykes."

In retrospect, Halsey was probably better at PSYOP than I was. I was a better shot, though.

So I whiled away the desultory hours by blasting the nearest neighbors of that school with my impassioned Arabic plea to get out the vote. We didn't care who they voted for. The victory, in this benighted, septic political backwater, was to vote at all. No one waved, stopped what they were doing, or in any way acknowledged the loony blaring appeals to democracy over

---

[25] No Roll messages directed Iraqi nationals not to drive during the elections. This was to cut down on the incidence of mobile car bombs.

their rooftops. The streets were empty except for three kids in their mum's little house, across from the school entrance. She was a pretty thing, young and probably a widow. The kids would wave shyly, open up in a grin, then dart behind their mother's skirts. I goofed around some, hot-miking clumsy Arabic greetings at the kids. Their young mother looked stolidly at the ground, but she didn't pull her kids inside. Maybe she would vote.

Somebody had to.

"It'll be a miracle if we get fifty people in here to vote," I told anyone who would listen. The Iraqi commandos up on the roof with me grinned and nodded.

"Your mother and I had a high old time last night," I added. They grinned and nodded some more. I wondered what they were saying about me.

"*Stock-BELLI-coom!*," I screamed. *That* got them going. Means something along the lines of "go vote!" Well, I thought so, anyway. We all screamed it a few times, grinning like devils. Many thumbs were up.

Just like U.S. special ops guys, Iraqi commandos implicitly know they're great looking and intelligent, many notches above their peers. They implored me to upgrade my messages, which referenced the Iraqi National Guard (since folded into the army); they wanted messages specifically telling the people of Tall 'Afar that the election sites would be secured by the heroes called "commandos." I found a commando lieutenant who spoke passable English, and we laid a couple of messages onto the DVR/MP3 that I'd borrowed from the Air Force JTAC[26] who shared a bunker office with us.

The army didn't give us the gear that we needed, but what army ever did? You go to war with the army you've got, soldiers are fungible but gear is expensive and G-D bless St. Rumsfeld, patron saint of richly endowed contractors.

The vanity did not end there. Every last commando had to get his picture taken. Pretty soon, my digital camera was toast, and I had one pair of batteries left for the election itself. So I just kept punching the button on my lifeless camera, gazing thoughtfully at the dead, black display, then giving them the thumbs up.

They loved it. They trust Americans: our friendliness, our sincerity, our faultless technology.

In case you're wondering, the army didn't issue the team a Nikon digital camera, either. My wife did. It had a lot of miles on it when it got back to her. Good thing we popped for the extended warranty.

Seems you can't get one for marriages, though. Not even new batteries, come to that.

One thing that wasn't about to go dead was the loudspeaker. I had packed an extra forty pounds or so of BA5590s, the army's all-purpose radio battery that we also used for our speaker, into my ruck.

---

[26] The Joint Tactical Air Controller is an air force enlisted member responsible for coordinating aviation missions from the ground. Pronounced "jay-tack".

With 80 or more pounds of "manpack" over my body armor, two grenades, eleven full mags, GPS, knife, buddy aid kit, carabineers, and candy for the kiddies, I needed both hands and feet to tote my rig up the crude concrete stairs leading to the rooftop. Not to mention "Darth Helmet," the five-pound *coup de grace* in discomfort that only Reservists and Guard guys wore by then. "Real" soldiers got the new, lighter, better suspended Modular Integrated Communications Helmets. The MICH was said to have several times the ballistic protection of our old school K-pots. But, ours not to bitch and cry, ours but to do and… never mind that part.

And so we squawked on, the commandos and I, trading lunches and punches and bilingual insults. I taught a couple of them what the safety on the AK47 was for, something that was curiously important to me. Those guys walked all over the place and pointed their weapons every which way. They all wanted to look through my optic, which was fine until one handsome bubba nearly dropped my rifle over the edge of the roof. That was the end of weapons familiarization. A fine time was had by all.

I knew damn well it was a complete waste of time. No one would come. A theater-wide boondoggle. But down in the lobby, they kept prepping tally boxes and stacking ballots, shaking up purple ink and going quietly, urgently down their checklists. And two rooftops over, Charger's gunners were stacking ammo cans next to their machine gun position.

Election Day dawned overcast and cool. When I got up in the dark, in a side room that had been taken over by first squad, third PLT, Apache Company—grunts on loan to the cavalry—Tall 'Afar was virtually silent. No cars had been allowed on the streets for three days, and there wasn't a city sound to be heard that you'd recognize: only chickens, empty *ghee* cans rattling along ahead of the lonesome wind, and the sound of first prayer call wailing out, louder than my manpack and with centuries more staying power in the message.

On our third morning there, we rose up cold and stiff out of a smelly pile of bodies and scraped disposable razors over our stubble, picked through breakfast bars and Gatorade, stumbled out for a piss. Not a creature was stirring but a few grimy joes.

As the sun rose, so did the gunfire. Harassing fire from Ali Baba started early, and made us skip smartly along when crossing the parking area between the school and hospital. I joined a Stryker patrol on Charger Six's vehicle.

We rolled through Tall 'Afar's nearby neighborhoods, not looking for a fight but finding several.

The commandos who were dismounted in the same area had a tendency to utilize what I called the "Reverse Polish Firing Squad" battle drill: they'd form into a circle, face out and blaze away in all directions. Our infantry—which didn't practice it—called this 360-degree tactic the "Death Blossom."

Iraqis with AKs were hell-for-brave, though. I lurked in the air guard hatch (convenient for ducking), securing the captain and scanning alleyways.

An Iraqi male poked his head out; I pointed my rifle at him and gestured. He poked his head out again and I buried a 5.56mm round in the front wall of his house about a foot over his head, ending his curiosity. This happened several times.

Usually with women, you only had to wave them in. Young guys were hardheads, though. It's the same all over the world.

One *hajji*, about 200 meters down, kept looking around the corner, scanning, then withdrawing. A warning shot didn't do it for this kid. A second warning shot chipped brick within two feet of his head. He looked again. The next time I saw him, he was trotting across the alleyway, toward the commandos' position.

He was dressed in black. He was carrying something. It looked like an AK.

No pressure.

When the bullet smacked him, he went straight down. It was very non-theatrical. I wasn't sure I'd hit him; it looked like he'd tripped.

I didn't shoot again. Two people—not dressed in black, not carrying anything—ran out and dragged him back to where he'd started, at the corner.

I didn't shoot them.

"What was that?!" The Stryker soldiers down below were hackled. Couldn't really blame them.

"Warning shot."

It came out calmly, this lie. I was a support soldier. A nice guy, there to help. I didn't shoot people. I warned them, fair and square. It was a warning shot.

Then we got into gear, and rumbled off another block or two. CPT Halsey, busy on the radio, had never looked up from his maps.

We linked up with the troop XO a couple of blocks over. He was stopped outside a home, with more detainees and casualties than he could tote in his truck. We took on four detainees. They squatted on the floor nuts to butts, flex-cuffed to the front. Most times, we cuffed them behind their backs only if they were violent.

Charger 6's terp eyed his countrymen like they might attack at any moment. Our Stryker instantly reeked of sweet cologne over well-developed human body spice, crossed with fear-pressed urine.

"There's a civilian casualty in the house. Have you got a litter?," asked the El-Tee.

There came a burst of AK fire from down the alley, and he yarded out his nine-mil to blast a few shots in the general direction, shooting gang banger-style with his hand tipped flat.

"Fuckers!," he yelled, then holstered his weapon and grinned at me, waggling his eyebrows. Spirits were high. Ammo was free.

We had a litter. I broke it out. 1LT Bonney and I headed into the house, clearing it muzzle-first. Inside the house, a young man lay on the floor. He was wearing shorts and a t-shirt, without even the ubiquitous plastic sandals. This was January, and the temperature was probably in the mid-40s, Fahrenheit. I wondered where his clothes had gone.

He was a military-age male. I wondered if he'd been dressed in black that day.

The wound in his abdomen looked like maybe a liver shot. His eyes were glazed. We slung him onto the sled—he might have weighed 130 pounds, if he'd worn heavier clothes—

and loaded him into the commander's Stryker, tucking him onto the right-side crew seat. Crouching and looking around curiously, his father came aboard behind him and curled down onto the floor.

Full house.

A detainee had shit himself into his man dress, and the wounded man bled out onto the crew seat. Somebody prayed quietly in Arabic, another protested his innocence in broken English from his wobbly perch atop a bag filled with cheap Chinese rifles—including the one taken off him on a rooftop. A complete menagerie: like Noah's ark, if it were launched from the Tower of Babel to sail through Hell.

The wounded man had three blue dots tattooed onto his ankle. I asked the commander's big-eyed terp what it meant: was it a terrorist marking?

"No, for... for beauty."

His wound was a clean shot, through and through. We dressed him quickly with simple gauze padding, and sped toward the hospital. I tried not to step on him as the Stryker lurched around corners and I banged my ribs off the sides of the air guard hatch, tiptoeing on the edge of the seat that held the wounded man while scanning for targets on rooftops and down alleyways.

We knocked a piece off a building corner with the fat-hipped slat armor and didn't slow down. We had no medic along. A soldier down in the crew compartment held the edge of the litter up so my bleeder wouldn't roll off onto the floor.

He was dead within minutes. The father's expression didn't change, though he never stopped looking at his son's face.

He was looking at eternity in that moment, and he couldn't see us at all.

When we dropped ramp at the hospital, the terp helped me carry the dead man inside. Iraqi doctors slung him up onto an emergency table, right off the slag-strewn foyer. His father watched stoically while they performed thumping, violent chest compressions at the rate of about 90 per minute. It looked like they were trying to beat him back to life, to punish him for dying.

I wanted to teach them proper CPR. I wanted to yell at them to stop, leave him alone, quit beating on his scrawny, dead chest.

About the kid he killed in Mosul a few weeks earlier, our bachelor detachment commander had told Big Danny, "It was a good shooting.

"You're in the clear."

Big Danny, father of three, had replied, "You don't fuckin' get it, sir."

Standing in the crunchy hallway of an underlit hospital, I looked at the father of the insurgent on the table and wished I didn't get it, either. I wouldn't know what to do with his forgiveness, but I'll never know what to do without it.

CPT Halsey had warned me not to leave the litter behind.

"We're running out of 'em."

So I asked for the green canvas litter back, and collected a couple more that had piled up in the hallways. The doctors stared hard at me as I carried out the litters. CPT Halsey's terp backed carefully out under his oversized blue helmet, afraid to turn his back.

Gunfire was intensifying around the voting center by then. There had been a couple of significant explosions within a couple of clicks, which still sent up rich, black roils of smoke. I gave CPT Halsey back his litters, and picked up my speaker pack. For about 20 minutes, as Charger troopers blasted concrete fragments off a beautifully finished luxury home across the MSR and the AK fire skipped around us, I broadcast my pro-election spiel over a masonry wall near the school.

The voters trickled in.

They walked, most of them, with the dignity of righteous action. One voter was shot in the belly. By his own insistence, he was carried into the polling place to vote before being carried across the lot under fire to the hospital. I guess they let him jump the line.

Some ran, ducking and holding their headpieces but coming anyway. Coming to vote.

I took a break from broadcasting to run a few boxes of 7.62mm linked-belt ammo for the machine gunners, who were having way too good a time, then got back on my squawk box.

The squadron commander rolled up in his personal, hotrod Stryker. He was waving at me. I waved back. He waved harder. Friendly fella.

1LTBonney trotted over, ducking the fire.

"Rattlesnake Six says shut that thing off!"

"What?!" I had plugs stuffed into my ringing ears.

"*TURN IT OFF!* Colonel Pingel says you're just pissing 'em off!"

"The fuck does he know?"

"Just turn it off!"

"Roger, sir."

Guess I didn't convince *him*: negative impact indicator for that PSYOP mission. Back to the unemployment line.

A lot of good men thought that LTC Pingel was an egotistical, hardheaded idiot, a nepotism beneficiary who couldn't find his ass with both hands and a flashlight on a clear day and who cared about nothing more than grubbing for his star, but how would I know about that?

I was just a staff sergeant. I shut it down.

Since I now officially had nothing left to do, I rejoined my adopted infantry squad to patrol the nearby streets on foot, looking for shooters who were targeting voters. I took along my digital camera. We waved and smiled at the voters, then crossed the MSR over to where we'd been receiving fire from. I put my camera away and brought my rifle to low ready.

Just a straphanger, I tagged along and pulled rear security for them. I hated walking backward, but as an old broody hen who should have been home with my own kid, it seemed like the place for me.

We got nothin'.

Policed up some AK brass from an intersection, tactically questioned a couple of guys, and neutralized no one. We did figure out that the gunfire was coming down the alley on an angle, and that Charger's two-forty gunners were shooting at hallucinations, but that wasn't a huge surprise. They were just having a good time up there, rocking the gun. Every time a round or two came down, they'd cheerfully burn through a belt and a half in response.

We spent a lot of your money that day.

Our little patrol shut down the constant AK fire, though. The rest of the city was a hodge-podge of scattered gunfire and the occasional big, black, smoky boom, but the consistent fire from across the way was stopped. After that, it was just sporadic, hit and run stuff. One Stryker gunner had the charging handle of his .50-cal. shot off in front of his face, but he was lucky. No Purple Heart for him that day. Eye pro *rules!*

And the voters rolled in.

They came from all over the city. They came with their children and donkeys and wives. I look at the pictures now and can still hardly believe the lines. Thousands of Iraqis, holding up their proud, purple fingers. Women, bandaged head to foot in their *burkas*, voting for the first time in their lives. Venerable old men voting in maybe their second real election. Young, hip guys in sharp Western suits. Farmers in grubby *dish-dashas*. Donkey carts and favorite dogs. My favorite shot was of an old man, his young son and his old wife, all giving me the finger in lurid, living purple.

It was a sight to see.

It went on and on. Twelve thousand people voted in Tall 'Afar that day, and each of them had to risk their life to do it. People in my precinct wouldn't go to vote if there was heavy traffic.

I hadn't voted in person in years. That was what absentee ballots were for, right? Right then and there, I resolved to go the following year, if only to shake the palsied hand of the old bat manning the booth. She had suddenly become one of my heroes.

I would fly home to a state that gave up setting out polling stations. Too inconvenient. Too expensive. Nobody cared.

By 0200, we had policed up hundreds of spools of concertina wire and thrown them onto enormous tractor-trailers. The trucks were packed up, fueled, ready to go. The ballot boxes—precious cargo—were sealed and loaded, held under guard. I sat in the Charger commander's Stryker again, too bone-tired to move. The radio squawked, but I ignored it until CPT Halsey sighed.

"It's going to be awhile longer."

"What's up, sir?"

"We have to wait and secure the HETS.[27] Should be about forty more minutes."

"You know, we really did something here today, sir."

I rolled my head around to the sound of crackling neck bones.

"At least, I think we did."

"Yeah. Let's hope they can take it from here. This country needs to carry its own water next time."

I lit up a smoke, unauthorized in military vehicles, and sucked on it until my eyes itched too much to want to close. The captain looked at me.

---

[27] Heavy Equipment Transport System. See "enormous tractor-trailers," above.

"It was something, though, wasn't it?"

"A sight to see, sir."

And so we waited there, wakeful but bleary, until we headed back to the FOB around 0530 and made it to the DFAC before it closed at 0800. That had to be the best KBR chow I ever ate.

I'd been up for thirty-some hours by the time I got back to my hooch. It didn't feel historical, not then. Like most of the joes, most of the time, I was just tired.

My knees burned. My back ached. My eyeballs itched with harsh corneal fur. I cared only about ripping the batteries out of the manpack, filing my report and staggering off to the rack. That night, I ran another mission with another unit—a cordon and search, probably—and the night after that, and the night after that, with daytime Battle Update Briefings in between.

I didn't think about Election Day again until much later.

I'm really not sure what I think of it now. Of my experiences in Iraq, this was the hardest to parse. It wasn't the best of days or the worst of days. There were elements of both. In some ways it was a high point, a kind of crisis in the harem-scarem plotline of that scattershot war.

Or peacekeeping operation. Or counter-insurgency. Whatever we call it these days when we task our Department of Defense to kill folks overseas as a policy statement. It's an active sort of defense.

In other ways, it was just another day at the office. I formed no tidy thoughts about what my teammate called "Game

Day," except maybe for this one: the good guys didn't win, and the bad guys didn't win.

At least that one time, the home team won.

TOOLS OF THE TRADE

For even the high lifted and chivalric Crusaders of old times were not content to traverse two thousand miles of land to fight for their holy sepulchre, without committing burglaries, picking pockets, and gaining other pious perquisites by the way.

Had they been strictly held to their one final and romantic object—that final and romantic object, too many would have turned from in disgust.

—Herman Melville, *Moby Dick*

It was hours before the first call to prayer when I woke up for the fourth time that night, burned my eyes on the Luminox dial, shoved old feet into cold boots and stood up quiet in the darkness, listening. I heard generators running.

I put a hand out to the right and found my rifle and body armor, another out to the left for the big MOLLE[28] ruck

_____

[28] A system for securing gear to the body or to other gear.

that served as my nightstand. In the absolute dark of my blinds-drawn hooch, I could find my DCU blouse, bleached to a smeary light butterscotch, by the 0230 glow of my watch. I slipped it over my Under Armour tactical tee. On its best day, the issue cotton undershirt was only good for cleaning weapons.

Forty-five seconds later, I was dressed and shrugging into my "tool belt," an Interceptor Body Armor vest. The front was a MOLLE-strapped rack crowded with the khaki- and green-colored tools of my trade: bullet pouches, compass, fixed-blade knife, medical pack, whistle, night vision goggles, surgical scissors, switchblade knife, digital camera, multi-tool, more ammunition. It cantilevered enough weight out front to make my 40 year-old back creak, but it would be counterbalanced by a big rucksack soon enough.

You can carry more ammunition than you need—and damn, it's heavy—but the instant you need ammo, you can't have too much. Cartridges are to line soldiers as clamps are to cabinetmakers: a pain in the rear to tote and store, but indispensable during those few, vital, fast-moving moments when you really, really need them.

I hung a Surefire G3 Nitrolon flashlight from a lanyard around my neck, careful not to mash the end cap button. Firing up 200 lumens of xenon light inside my little tuna can would blast my night vision for half an hour.

Then I clipped my Colt M4 rifle to the tactical sling on my vest, and started my commute to work.

Russ was already suited up and hopping around when I tapped softly on his door. Damn kid was always ready. There's no better tool in the world than a switched-on soldier.

A quick, preventive-maintenance visit to the stink box and off we schlepped, past boxcar-sized generator sets and sand-filled HESCO barriers[29] to the crenellated parking field dividing the TOC bunkers from our hoochal area. A quick shot from my Surefire showed me where each of the soldier-swallowing potholes lurked, all the way across the 150-meter parking zone.

The next best thing to a good troop is a functional coffeemaker, and Russ had Starbucks Breakfast Blend gurgling through our globetrotting Mr. Coffee before I could growl, "Where the Hell's my…"

Nothing cuts through the pasty phlegm of Iraq's "poo dust" like hot, fresh coffee. We sipped it quietly out of Styrofoam cups while we checked our gear.

Everything is disposable in a hostile fire zone.

My big toolbox for the day was a PSYOP speaker pack. At 75 lbs., it was handy for broadcasting, not so handy to tote. I sighed as I pulled BA5590 batteries—each the size and weight of a brick—off the charger and added spares to my pack. On the far side of the bunker, Russ loaded up on visual product: handbills and posters and cards, oh my.

Finishing up our coffee, we stuffed gear into Elsa the Wonderhummer and rolled across the retired Saddam airbase to our supported infantry company. We reported at the appointed hour of 0330 and Apache's commander threw us aboard his XO's Stryker armored vehicle. We were only straphangers, but

---

[29] Quickly erected, anti-ballistic revetments made from canvas-lined wire cages and filled with sand by front-end loaders.

Apache's ground pounders were grunts orphaned on a cavalry base. They shared our doom-struck sense of humor. We got on well with them.

On any job site, first impressions are important. My speaker bag was too big to stow inside the crew compartment—if you wanted to stow any soldiers in there, that is. It always got lashed to the roof. Whenever we rolled with a new gaggle of guys, I'd one-arm press the speaker pack up to an air guard and casually ask, "Couldja grab this for me?" When it damn near sucked him over the side, I'd boost it up to him. Then I'd make a crack about us PSYOP types putting the "T" in S-O-F, and we'd all get along fine after that. I may have invested a bit too much shoulder cartilage in that little trick. The new troop commander emerged from his cluttered office, half-dressed with his armored vest on but no web gear.

"You all know what you're doing by now," he started. "Let's hear a word from Chaplain Goodall."

A hundred guys in green and tan armor, festooned with ammunition and buddy-aid kits, gave their attention to a barrel-chested chaplain with a fluty voice and a crooked, perpetual grin. Thirty-five years old with a couple of kids and an allegedly happy wife in Vancouver, the FOB Sykes chaplain was a prior-enlisted soldier and new school fundamentalist who had followed the Lord's call to Fort Lewis and ended up assigned to this cavalry squadron in a Stryker brigade.

"Okay, gather around guys," he said, fluttering his hands like a chorus line quarterback. "C'mon, bring it in."

The chaplain was going to call our next move from the playbook of God.

"The first thing I want to tell you men," the chappy began, "is that God doesn't have a problem with killing, as long as it's righteous killing and the killing is performed with justice and in the glorification of His name."

A few soldiers looked up, puzzled, as CPT Goodall plowed on in his sunny voice.

"God doesn't have a problem with killing bad guys. For Bible-believing Christians, God is all *about* killing bad guys.

"Now let's bow our heads and pray together.

"Most heavenly Father, Ye who shielded the Israelites in their travails and strengthened Joshua to blow down the wicked walls of Jericho, we ask You to make your holy presence manifest in the hearts of these your soldiers. Make a mighty shield to guard them in their missions, and blunt the swords of thine enemies…"

This went on for some time. Eventually, my neck got stiff and I straightened up to look around. A few helmets and patrol caps were still bowed, but most were staring blankly as though they could see straight through the hangar blast doors to the green image of a target waiting in the dark.

"…and let them strike another tremendous blow for peace and justice in Your name, Lord. This we ask in the strong name of your son Jesus Christ, who taught us to pray…"

That was our cue to chant the Lord's Prayer together. Black, white or Latino; Catholic, Presbyterian or Muslim—no surveys were taken. Like the Pledge of Allegiance, the Lord's Prayer was brand-independent ecumenicalism endorsed by the chain of command, now new and improved by a martial intro worthy of the most militant Pakistani *madrasa*.

Our huddle broke on the final "amen" as quickly as cheers drown the last note of the national anthem at baseball games. Lieutenants accosted the captain while sergeants broke off to check on their men and equipment, administering clipped imperatives about more temporal concerns:

"Pull those jerry cans off the back. It's a fire hazard,

dumbass."

"Did you fill radios?" [30]

"You can piss later. Yeah, alright, hurry up."

"Get that FBCB2 up *now!* You shouldn't've been fuckin'
off in the first place!"

"How much ammo we got for the fifty?"

Soon enough, we were all sitting in the half-lit bellies of
our assigned vehicles, running through checklists in our heads
while subconsciously monitoring the radio speakers' jargoned
mumble: "Apache Six-Seven, Six-Six."

"Six-Seven. Send it."

"Line up on the road. SP one-zero mikes."

"Roger." The first sergeant switched from command to
troop net. "All vehicles move to the gate."

Cables groaned and ramps clanged heavily into place all
over Apache's parking ramp. Supercharged diesels spooled up
and soldiers on bench seats bumped shoulders as their armored
transports lurched into motion.

Most Apache guys were dead sick of riding air guard, so
I could usually talk someone out of his hatch without pulling
rank. I put a dirty boot on the troop seat and hoisted my tired ass
up into the air guard hatch. It was better than being inside if
somebody puked up a festering gobbet of poo dust, unsanitized
black water, KBR niblets and powdered green Gatorade.

You made a fine target silhouetted against the Big Sky
moon of northwestern Iraq, but there wasn't much better than
riding air guard in a Stryker blasting down deserted highways in
the dark, senses turned up to 11, the only source of heat and

---

[30] The radio fill is a data burst of cryptographic information that allows
the radio to communicate with other U.S./allied radios. If its fill is not
current, a tactical radio will transmit and receive only in the clear.

noise and motion in all the world. Some bikers believe that only motorcyclists know why a dog hangs its head out the car window. I submit that they've never pulled air guard in the sandbox.

Testing my NVGs for the third time, I pulled a drive-on rag over my nose and mouth and pulled out my first full magazine, laying it on the cold steel roof next to the rifle I held loosely by its grip, waiting for the VC's command to go "red-direct" as we left the wire. God willing, I would stuff it back into my ammo pouch at end of mission still pregnant with its lightning potential of powder, brass and copper-jacketed lead.

Deliver us from evil.

In any trade, tool prep separates retail hobbyists from the pros. Before we lifted off from Ft. Bragg, my team disassembled all our rifle magazines, cleaned and tested them, and reassembled them with 550 cord loops extending from the base plates. Beyond giving employment to our jittery fingers, we now knew we could reliably yank mags out of our pouches by the cords. We could also snap our empties onto a carabineer during firefights.

In a combat zone, nothing is expendable.

After checking in with the Apache squaddies holding Tall 'Afar castle, a 1,400 year-old tool of the Ottoman occupation, we wound downhill through the cobbled streets to the road beneath its east-facing wall. Morning prayer call was starting by the time we dropped ramp and moved out on LPCs[31] to our objective, a group of dwellings thrown together as haphazardly as a pile of stone puppies.

The staff sergeant leading the patrol had his mission, and we had ours. He proceeded to interview people with his

---

[31] Leather Personnel Carriers: a slang acronym for combat boots.

HUMINT[32] specialist while Russ and I set up a series of rooftop locations to broadcast counter-terror and non-interference messages from our pack's portable amplifier, speaker and digital recorder. The grunts carried a battering ram and a 12-gauge in case persons of interest didn't come out when they knocked, and we broadcast recorded Arabic messages in case others wouldn't go back in—persuasion added to coercion.

"How do we know they're even listening?," Russ asked at one point. Two hundred meters away, a crowd gathered, pointing and yelling.

"Play Message Three."

Message Three was an order to disperse and go inside, or be detained. Everyone went inside but the two military-aged males who liked to yell. I pointed my rifle in their general direction, just to scope them a little closer through the 4X ACOG sight. The two fellas looked a little agitated. Then they looked at me. Then they went inside.

Around mid-morning, the squad we supported finished their door knocking. We quit our roof hopping and rejoined them to finish out their patrol.

Moving along the river was a hands-on, squishy-boot education in every needed thing that's missing in Iraq, and every blight we hoped to remove. Tall 'Afar didn't exactly have a garbage dump; instead, the whole town functioned as one. Citizens pushed and slung everything from cars to cans to kitchen slop over the edge, out the window, down the hill. Woe betide those who lived low on the topography.

---

[32] Human Intelligence Gatherers were field interrogators.

By the time it slumped to the river, Tall 'Afar's garbage was a viscous stew of offal, flaps of plastic, moldy textiles and sewage. Constantly outgassing, the boiling grey river occasionally caught fire.

Our tools were rifles and machine guns. What we really needed were shovels. Wishing for a decent hardware store like Hardwick's, where I had worked back in Seattle, I stepped around a dog carcass and slipped on a chunk of fruit. Stumbling for a balance point, I heaved my ruck around and crunched my downhill boot through the ribcage of a rotting donkey.

Damn. Those were the best boots I had left.

From the river, we moved up across the crotch of the road where it started to rise out of the drainage. There was a large building there, like a warehouse or barn that I'd been wondering about. I grabbed Russ out of our Ranger file and pulled him toward it. One of the infantrymen told me they'd already searched the building.

"Staff Sarn't Salinas says we don't go in there today."

"Tell your staff sergeant that Staff Sergeant Lewis will be out in a moment."

"Whatever."

It was dead quiet in the building. When we yanked the squealing steel door open to infiltrate the place, we walked into a working museum of woodcraft. Dust motes swirled through shafts of sunlight falling onto a monstrous iron bandsaw, wide board jointer, and a planer that could flatten totem poles.

Several benches were set up around a workshop bursting with finished and partially complete furniture, mostly cabinets and dressers. Narrowly dovetailed drawers were wrapped by

chisel-cut mortise and tenon casework. Hand carvings
embellished edges and panels, some surfaces further bedecked by
punched metal detailing.

We were surrounded by the hope of life.

Russ watched me curiously as I walked around, quietly
touching things. I moved the top wheel of the colossal bandsaw,
stroked my fingertips over the jointer's worn outfeed surfaces.
Decades of use had left them nearly devoid of Blanchard
grinding swirls. Not a power tool in there was younger than me.

"Hey, Sergeant, look over here."

I walked across the shop to where Russ stood over a
workbench. Except for the thick coating of dust, it looked like
the joiner had laid down his tools and gone to lunch. *Chai* and
deep-fried eggs, maybe, or falafel with goat's milk. Work locally,
eat locally.

I plucked a hand tool out of a pile of curly shavings.
There was a half-inch #39 dado plane lying next to it, but my eye
was caught by a No. 5 Bailey pattern.

"Russ, ya know what this is called?" I grinned like I
hadn't grinned in months. "This is a 'jack plane'."

"It's named after you, Sergeant!" Russ's eyes sparkled,
reflecting the avarice in my own. "You should put it in your
pack."

I frowned at Russ, then down at the tool in my hands. It
felt right there, broken in but not busted up. The sole was
conditioned, the iron had plenty of meat, and the tote tucked as
smoothly into my hand as a river stone into King David's sling.
Muscle memory kicked in. I field stripped the plane, popped off

the cap iron and squinted straight on at the edge. The user kept a fair hone on his equipment.

"You should just take it, Sarge."

I stood there, thinking about it. We never took property. Souvenir hunting makes U.S. forces look bad and militarizes the populace. Not incidentally, stealing is wrong. But here was this wondrous thing—this fine tool deserving of use—just sitting there calling out to every tool jones I had, a pretty pruning hook in a world bristling with spears.

It was a red Marples. The finish was perfect.

Red Marples handplanes haven't been made for ages. They were never imported to the States. It's nearly impossible to score one in the U.S.A. Back at the hardware store, we had talked about them in hushed tones, plotting our acquisitions.

The voice in my head agreed with Russ. I'd probably never hold another red Marples in my own two hands if I left that one behind. That felt like justification enough.

There was room in my pack. It wouldn't hurt my knees any worse than the gear already in there. Hell, I could toss out a BA5590, call it a field loss and be at even weight.

Its owner was probably dead. At the least, he wouldn't be back here anytime soon. Overwatched by the guns of the U.S. cavalry on the hilltop, this shop stood at the edge of one of the nastiest insurgent neighborhoods in that whole benighted republic. That wouldn't change anytime soon. There was no electricity to power the big iron.

The Turcoman who pushed this plane surely didn't know what he had here. It was a plain working tool to him, bench clutter; a donkey to beat on until it failed, then unsentimentally chuck into the slough of despond down by the riverside.

I looked at that plane, snuggled into my hands, and wished for that simple thing as hard as I've ever wished for an object. Reassembling it, I carefully aligned the chip breaker a millimeter back from the edge. My weapon hung forgotten at my side as I took a few imaginary strokes. In my mind's eye, ribbons of Port Orford cedar sussurated off the frame of the Aleutian kayak project water-dancing through my desert dreams.

Then I set the red Marples carefully back on the bench, side down to protect the iron, and walked out into the sun.

When you take a man's money, you steal a piece of his time. If he has time enough left and uses it well, he can outbalance your pilfering with his skill. If you nick a man's tools, you remove hard-won extensions of his faculties, muscles and nerves. Though I might have convinced myself to take a trophy, I couldn't cut off the hands of a craftsman. That's not American justice.

That handplane would have called me thief every time I touched it. Maybe I'd have a red Marples someday, but not until I earned it fair.

If one day I am so blessed, every time I use it I'll think of a lean, dark woodworker holding his beard out of tool's way as he sweats over his grandfather's bench in an antique cabinet shop, on a battle-torn street, just uphill from where the river runs with fire.

Prosper well, my brother.

WE HAVE MET THE ENEMY

As they narrated to each other their unholy adventures, their tales of terror told in words of mirth; as their uncivilized laughter forked upwards out of them, like the flames from the furnace; as to and fro, in their front, the harpooneers wildly gesticulated with their huge pronged forks and dippers; as the wind howled, and the sea leaped, and the ship groaned and dived, and steadfastly shot her red hell further and further into the blackness of the sea and the night, and scornfully champed the white bone in her mouth, and viciously spat round her on all sides; then the rushing Pequod, freighted with savages, and laden with fire, and burning a corpse, and plunging into that blackness of darkness, seemed the material counterpart of her monomaniac commander's soul.

—Herman Melville, *Moby Dick*

"Man, this sucks *ass*," said the machine gunner in the other air guard hatch. "I thought it was s'posed to be *hot* over here."

"Wait a few weeks," I answered. "We'll be toasty.

"Want some coffee in the meantime? Should still be warm."

I had drained an urn of scalding hot coffee into my thermos at about 0300, and it was only mid-morning.

"No, thank you, Sergeant," the PFC said, recovering his manners for no perceptible reason. "I don't really drink coffee."

A few snowflakes drifted down to collect on his sleeves and weapon. I looked up into the hard gray sky, then back at him, and smiled.

"Not even when Hell freezes over?"

"Hey, I'll take some of that coffee if you've got some left, Sergeant Lewis," came the lieutenant's voice through the CVC ear cups.

"Comin' at ya, sir."

I ducked down into the hatch and passed my thermos up forward. Outside the Stryker, there was another short burst of AK fire. Popping my head up, I found the 240 gunner leaning into his weapon but not obviously concerned.

"Same guy?," I asked.

"Yup."

"Somebody tell that idiot to stop shooting!," ordered our lieutenant from up in the hatch.

It's good to get your blood moving on a cold day, and I'd already performed my PSYOP straphanger mission, taking a three-question survey of 200 people waiting in the walk-up line at the benzene station. There were another several hundred behind them, waiting patiently for the station to be open for a few hours.

Neither scarcity nor novelty ever lose their fascination. Here in the country with the world's second or third largest petroleum reserves, whole families camped out overnight to buy a bucket of go-juice to light their stoves. Back home, only a Star Wars movie or a concert by wizened elder statesmen of rock could inspire such sacrifice.

In accordance with tradition, the station owners would gouge individual purchasers far above the posted rate, which was set by the government. They would also sell to the black marketeers first, unofficial middlemen pulling tank trailers behind their farm tractors. The gas pirates would buy a couple hundred gallons at the subsidized rate to resell in side streets, pocketing a hefty profit less the substantial protection money paid to the Farhat tribe, whom we mostly referred to as "insurgents."

The Farhat gunmen worshiped Mammon primarily, and were insurgents in the tasty causes of profit and tribal vengeance. They were experts at vengeance and no slouch at the protection racket, either.

All of which brought us downtown on a Tuesday afternoon to overwatch the fuel station. Actually, because this was a combined op, we weren't really overwatching the fuel patrons or keeping order there. Instead, we were overwatching the Iraqi National Guard so that hopped-up Farhat shooters wouldn't destroy them while they stood around picking their noses and pointing AK-74s at the crowds they were assigned to protect.

One ING on the north side of the station, unusually chubby, was growing frustrated with the crush of the crowd.

When Iraqis with guns become frustrated, they shoot into the air. In their worldview, the bullets will never come down. Maybe Allah catches them.

When Iraqis are overjoyed, they also shoot into the air. When confused, they shoot into the air. When faced with an enemy force, God only knows where they might shoot. Occasionally someone is killed, *insh'Allah*.

"I'll go talk to him, sir," I answered over the intercom. "C'n I borrow your terp?"

"Hell, yeah," he said. "Thanks, Sergeant Lewis."

"No prob'm, sir."

I asked the 240 kid to overwatch me, and he obligingly dropped the ramp so I could dismount with Dagwood. All our terps had Americanized nicknames, and Dagwood was a skinny little *hajji* who had been named for his prodigious appetite. We walked 200 meters to the guard's position, where the situation was degenerating.

The guard had lost the respect of the customers, who were now shoving forward over the control line and practically daring him to shoot them—and he looked like he was ready to cap a few citizens in the name of civil order. His muzzle was pointed straight into the crowd and you could see the egg whites of his eyes at fifty meters.

"*A'salaam aleikum*," I said, patting my heart.

He glanced at me, then back at his antagonists. "*Aleikum salaam.*"

"Dagwood," I said, "tell him to stop shooting."

There was a brief exchange in Arabic, then Dagwood told me, "He says they are not in his control. They will not listen. He must control them from the pushing."

Easing the guard's muzzle down to point at the ground, I looked at the crowd. They looked back, curious. I wished for a GI closer to me than 200 meters, but there was nothing for it but to do it.

Sometimes, if you pretend to be an overwhelming force, people will take you at your word. Walking forward, I held my carbine at port arms and started pushing the biggest guy I could find back across the line. Then I walked along the face of the crowd, pushing people back, waving at the line on the ground, and yelling like a pissed-off football coach. They all stepped back. Some were even smiling a little at the crazy American.

Checking my six, I saw that our redoubtable Iraqi National Guardsman was pointing his weapon at the crowd again, safety off. That meant he was pointing his weapon at my back. I felt like killing him then and there, but that would have been the wrong message to send about social order and anyway, prison doesn't agree with me.

I walked back over, pointed his muzzle back down at the ground and pushed his rusted safety lever up to the SAFE position. Then I spoke quietly to Dagwood.

"Tell him to look at the crowd. See how many there are? How many bullets does he have? Can he shoot them all? Does he want to kill any of them?

I swept one hand toward the crowd. "These are Iraqis. There are children here.

"No more shooting."

A colorful argument ensued, with the ING trooper vociferously making his case to Dagwood. Terps weren't supposed to converse, they were supposed to interpret. Sometimes managing interpreters took more energy than it was worth. I cut in, asked, "What's the problem, Dagwood?"

Dagwood looked at me like he couldn't believe I was interrupting him. Couldn't I tell he had the situation under control?

"He said he must shooting, or no he can control them."

That was the precise argument heard so often against the "imposition" of democracy on Iraq: they *required* a strongman leader in order to function at any recognizable level of social order. This short-term view, convenient to isolationists, was advanced by everyone from insurgents to think tank academics, from political hacks to corrupt local cops to regional military leaders. All of them managed to ignore the bony finger of history, tapping gently on our collective shoulders to remind us that the self-rationalizing excuse used by every despot on record ought to be held in sharp suspicion by the free.

I squinted at the guy, and said very slowly out of the corner of my mouth, "Dagwood.

"Tell this dumb cock suckin' ass fuckin' son of a bitch that if he shoots one more time, I will take his weapon away from him. I will take his rifle back to my Stryker, and I will mail it home for a souvenir, and leave him here with *nothing*.

"No. More. Shooting."

"But he will be killed if he cannot have the gun!"

"*Insh'Allah*."

I turned my back on the Guardsman and stalked off toward our Stryker. Dagwood scampered to catch up. Before we got there, another burst of rounds exploded on the far side of the station. There were several more individual shots, and we saw our Stryker spool up and roar around the corner in a rooster tail of slushy street bilge.

Dagwood, a combat-experienced terp, trotted with me over to the station walls. We moved along partial cover to the shooting site, where a *jundi*[33] lay bleeding onto a poncho liner. His squad mates gestured around with wild eyes and a familiar lack of muzzle discipline.

"They say there was shot from long way away," Dagwood translated without being asked. "They shoot back."

Whenever ING had a negligent discharge—and they had great steaming shitloads of NDs—they always claimed to be responding to a shot from a long way off. This excuse was used even when they blew someone's belly out inside an armored vehicle. You had to wonder who they thought they could hit with a rarely cleaned AK at ranges of "long way away."

I eyeballed their casualty. His wounding started where the slug passed through the back meat of his left arm. It had subsequently traveled through the side of his vest, clean across his back and exited through his right chest, punching a second hole in the vest. Pretty good velocity for a bullet from a galaxy far, far away. I checked his fellow ING *jundis*. Every one of them had a

---

[33] "Jundi" is Arabic for "soldier." There was a distinct performance differential between Iraqi Army *jundis* and the Kurdish commandos.

steaming hot barrel from the fire spasm they'd indulged after the first shot felled their guy.

One of Apache Company's medics trotted up with his big, black medical pack and started rolling up Kerlix[34]. We shoved the casualty's faithful comrades, one of whom had probably just killed him, out of the way so he could be loaded up on a Stryker for CASEVAC. If he kept breathing until they got to FOB Sykes, our surgeons stood a decent chance of saving him from the vigilance of his brethren.

Another day at the office. We went back to our Stryker to wait out the last four hours of this mission.

"Leave any coffee for me, sir?

"No, man, I finished it."

I whiled away the rest of our on-station time by rationing out what wampum I had brought along—candy and school supplies, mostly, leavened by the occasional precious soccer ball—to kids who would come by to wave and grin at us.

We gave out Crayolas and little plastic backpacks and erasers, but no pencils. Pencils could be weapons.

We sometimes tossed MREs from the cases we kept on top of the Strykers. Cultural sensitivity dictated passing out *halal* rations, but those always went to Iraqi soldiers first. People in the villages got whatever came to hand: burritos, beef in spiced sauce, BBQ pork. What they can't read won't kill 'em, and Hell's probably no hotter than Muhollibiyah in late spring.

---

[34] Kerlix is medical gauze for packing wounds.

We hoarded water on long missions, but we'd give out leftovers when we were RTBing. Kids loved it when you mixed in the lime Gatorade powder packs from the mess hall. Young soldiers liked that goop, too. I always hated it.

Some young soldiers mixed up their extra lime Gatorade and tossed it to kids.

Some tossed them bottles of piss.

It wasn't long before LTC Pingel got tired of waiting for the populace to stop patronizing the car-and-tractor black market of the gasoline bandits. He had worked hard promoting the vigor of his exploits back up to brigade level, and it was no time to slack off his fiery leadership. With nary a pause to consider the situation—either tactically or socially—he saddled up his personal Stryker and headed downtown with blood, and benzene, in his eye.

The God of War was a fan of burning things. He was persuaded that crisped wreckage left a more lasting impression on the locals than an explosion, which—no matter how thumpingly robust—could only satisfy for the briefest instant. A burning car, truck or building would send up a black warning plume for hours. Burning the serfs' property let everyone know who was in charge. Smoke signals to Ali Baba. Burning up bad guys' property also provided better photo opportunities for the staff officers who tagged along on his forays.

The insurgents felt the same way, so they used the same tactics. Many smoky plumes rose over Tall 'Afar.

When the rolling royal court of Pingel's command element went out cruising for trouble, they usually found some. If there was none to be found, the colonel would create a situation. It was his sector. He could do what he wanted. And he had a functionally unlimited supply of thermite grenades.

Thus, when LTC Pingel's hunting party walked up on a semi-derelict taxicab to stop the owner from working on it and interrogate him, scarves tied onto the steering wheel were reason enough to presume that he was building an SVBIED. The man's effusive denials were enough in themselves to seal his conviction.

His car made a merry bonfire. A parade of staff pukes, happy to be out adventuring in large armored trucks, posed Rambo-style one after the other in front of the rapidly combusting subcompact, joking about toasting marshmallows. The *de facto* terror suspect was not detained—there were too many junketing officers on board, and no one wanted to sit next to his stinkin' *hajji* ass.

As we roared off to defend freedom and see if we could find a star for the colonel in a *wadi*[35] on the far side of town, the cabbie was still watching the fire, slack-jawed, arms at his side. That was one terrorist who would be walking to his next crime.

That'll teach him.

---

[35] A *wadi* is a ravine.

Cold or not, the gloves were off.

Patrolling one of the better neighborhoods among decently built homes and new construction, I felt my way from gate to gate barehanded so my good kangaroo and Nomex gloves wouldn't get gummed up with spray glue. Spray glue was our primary weapon system for bullseyeing hearts and minds. By the end of the evening, my hands would be black as usual, and I would spend the trip back rubbing hand sanitizer on them and picking the rubbery residue off my palms.

We were Reservists once, and young... The Reserves didn't get top-drawer equipment, and we didn't get much of the leftovers, either. Accordingly, my team was outfitted with one each obsolete AN/PVS-7B night vision device to go along with their obsolete team sergeant with my creaky knees, aching back and coffee-fouled temper. Two sets, leaving one of us to go without. I assigned one Seven-Bravo to Russ, since it's small help to have a machine gunner who can't see in the dark, and the other to Will for paper-hanging purposes.

"Sergeant, why don't you take them?"

"Don't worry about me," I told Will. "I'm blind as a bat any-damn-way."

So I felt my way down the coruscated walls and cap-screwed steel courtyard gates, easing along with gentle footfalls and stopping at each entrance to hang a few messages from America. Each time I raised my spray can, I felt for the tiny nozzle on its little white cap, turned that toward the wall and laid down some glue before smearing on a little piece of persuasion.

"We're not persuading anyone," Russ would say sometimes, out of earshot of our supported unit. "We're just combat paperboys.

"It would really suck to get killed handing out this shit."

I wasn't very reassuring to him on that point. "Everybody's gotta die of something," I cheerfully would remind him. "Long as we're here, may as well do it right."

I don't know who the hell I thought I was making sense to, but it probably wasn't him or me. Is it faith when you proceed on unknowable hopes—or when you know better but drive on anyway? I used to know, I thought then, but I couldn't remember anymore.

Mid-mission, I couldn't even remember why we'd come in the first place. All I could remember was how to perform our mission, and my enduring obligation to keep on dancing in circles, like a drunken, shambling bear. Progress was marked on the daily SITREP, in increments of thousands of bills posted, of hundreds of citizens addressed with a handshake and a smile under the gunfighter eyes of my overwatch.

If a wall said "POST NO BILLS" in Arabic, we would have posted over it. All graffiti was assumed to be hostile, unless it bore a product number from MNCI. The three of us would tear down enemy propaganda and replace it with friendly product (remember, kids, we don't do propaganda). Then a thousand gleeful delinquents would peel off our posters and run giggling to imported cells of Syrian insurgents with a pocketful of American candy and their beady little avaricious eyes peeled for the *jihad* of immediate convenience.

These Iraqis were out of their skulls. We weren't Johnny-come-lately invaders. This was no crusade of convenience. We had always been there. We would always be there. We were Exmochevco, we were BP with a drawl, Lawrence of Arabia with night scopes, drinking the Hatorade and drivin' on.

It would never be over, and no one would win. If the U.S.A. can't establish a worldwide caliphate, then who the hell can? Some billionaire son of the Saud? Hell, boy, our billionaires can beat the tar out of your billionaires. Just watch and see.

We'll never leave just 'cause you want us to.

But I was only a staff sergeant. Foreign policy flew miles above my pay grade. Not the tool pusher, just another tool. Sprayin' glue and flingin' poo. Moving to the next gate, I heard a soft thud followed by "Oof!" and a muffled curse.

Russ was standing in the middle of the street, but he was only two feet tall and I almost tripped over his head.

"Dude, what the fuck?"

"Can you help me out of here? My boots are all muddy."

His SAW was laying off to the side of the meter-deep hole he was standing in. In his deep-skirted Kevlar helmet with NVGs lashed to the front, Russ looked like a tiny alien being— "Darth Helmet"—or the sawed-off cartoon figure on a short-timer's calendar. I gave him an arm and heaved him out of the pit, and then laughed at him for having street sewage up to his crotch.

"You need to ride back on the roof," I said, then grabbed his Seven-Bravos, looked into the hole and almost pissed myself. I returned the NVGs to his groping paw in the dark and took a deep breath.

"Holy shit," I said. "Don't look down there."

"Why not?," he asked, and immediately looked. "Oh. Oh, my God."

"Yeah."

The pit, brimming with filth, was studded with vertical stakes of rebar. Their raw steel points were just visible above the reeking water surface. It was a miracle Russ hadn't been disemboweled, popped off a kneecap or torn out a femoral artery.

"Think it's a booby trap?"

We looked around. The whole street was torn up for a construction project that would undoubtedly go on for decades as local *sheikhs* pocketed their 90 percent skim of American sucker money.

"Nah, but you are one lucky sumbitch. Sure you're okay?"

"Can you hold my weapon?" I took his little machine gun, the propaganda video favorite of Abu Musab al Zarqawi, off his hands and he checked himself again, patting up and down each leg.

"Yeah, I'm good."

I pointed out a spot on the sidewalk, said, "Overwatch from right there."

I dug a small bottle of hand sanitizer out of my grenade pouch and and handed it to him.

"Make sure no one else falls in there."

Five minutes later, I mis-underestimated the aerosol can cap direction with numb fingers and foamed a layer of spray adhesive over both lenses of my glasses.

Now I was profoundly in the dark. Swiping furiously at them with the tail of my DCU shirt, I managed to rub a pair of small holes in the layer of rubber laminate I'd just created.

By then, it was time to head back to the truck so the Air Force could guide the Navy in to drop their bomb. The Army squadron commander wanted a show of force, so an FA-18 loitering 60 miles off had been called in to further destroy the junked car in a nearby *wadi*.

That'd teach those insurgents, by God. If Allah hadn't been such a corn-holing pussy, he'd have had air superiority.

Scanning the crew compartment yielded a count of minus one.

"Where's Mandeville?"

"I 'on't know—he was just here."

"Drop the ramp!"

I grabbed Russ's goggles and hunched back outside, scanned around and saw that Will had stopped across the road to decorate one more steel gate. There is such a thing as too much dedication to duty.

"Mandeville!" I was stage whispering, who knows why.

He peered over his shoulder at me through his spacey headgear. "What's up, sarn't?"

"Get back in the truck! They're dropping a bomb, dipshit!"

"Who's dropping a bomb?"

"Mount *up*, damn it! Gitcher fuckin' ass in the truck!"

Back in the belly of the Stryker with our butts on the hard crew seat and muzzles on the floor, I took stock of my little crew. Mandeville was just plain goofy as always, looking like a gangly teenager dressed up in his daddy's soldier clothes. Russ was dripping sewage, and I had vulcanized myself a pair of googly eyes.

"Well, that was amusing."

"Shit, I can't believe I missed all those stakes."

"What?," asked Will. "Who got steaks?"

"Just get up in the air guard hatch, Mandeville. You're gonna wanna see this."

Brief lightning flashed through the hatches as the ground attack fighter made a tracer-rich strafing run on his practice car. We heard the jet go booming around and set up for his next pass, talking constantly with our JTAC, then the flash and boom as he missed the money shot by 400 meters.

"Holy shit!," said Will, fumbling with his NVGs. "That was *sweet!*"

I looked across at Russ. He was a licensed pilot on the civilian side and loved everything about aircraft. "Your turn next time," I told him.

"That's okay," he said. "I wanted Mandeville to see it."

Rubbing hand sanitizer onto my fouled glasses with rubberized fingers, I manufactured a tight smile from my lips and eyebrows.

"Funny way to make a living, huh?"

The colonel's corpse fire was completely unintentional. He was just checking out a tip when things got weird.

In a shock to everyone's system, our local ING troopers had actually engaged a target. One of Allah's chosen, wobbling under the weight of his sacred suicide vest, emerged from between lines of stopped cars to rush their checkpoint. Everyone was surprised when they fired at him instead of dropping their rifles and running. The bomber was more startled than anyone. His briefing evidently hadn't included the contingency of getting plugged. Apparently, that whole 72-virgin deal is problematic for those who are shot down in the road before they can blow anyone up. Electing to express the better part of valor, he ran like a rabbit.

A badly overloaded rabbit.

Surprising everyone again, the ING actually hit him. Now no one knew what to do. Best call the Americans. The Americans would handle it.

When the God of War's Stryker skidded up to the scene, he had all current intel in hand, data-dumped straight into his ear over the secure net. He knew what had happened, he had a grid coordinate plotted, he knew the risk assessment on the ground, and best of all he knew that the EOD team would be busy for at least four hours reducing a pile of explosives left near Route Santa Fe on the north edge of town.

LTC Pingel knew just what to do.

A Civil Affairs senior NCO who was a frequent straphanger on the SCO's vehicle had brought along a digital video camera. He knew that memorable things tended to happen around cav officers, who were expressly interested in High Adventure. So SFC Gallagher recorded the scene that followed, and the video of it provided great hilarity around the FOB for weeks to come.

The colonel directed his vehicle to about 60 meters from where the bomber's body lay supine, just off the road. Proceeding to reduce the threat, he shot repeatedly into the corpse with his rifle. On the video, the carbine shots sounded dull: *pop, pop, pop... pop.*

On the VCD, you could hear the colonel cuss the corpse for not blowing up. He asked SFC Gallagher for more magazines and reloaded his carbine. Someone less important would clean his weapon for him later.

The bomb-wired carcass soaked up half a magazine of 5.56mm rounds before starting to whistle like a boiling kettle. The video shows a nearly invisible flame distorting the air around the corpse for a few seconds before the body vaporizes with a concussive bang. Evidently, the AIF armorer crafted an effective vest after all. It just needed a sure hand at the detonator to go off all at once.

In the suicide field, good help is hard to find. Also, employee retention is miserable.

ING troopers found the bomber's flash-fried head more than a hundred meters off. Islam requires reverent handling of the dead, but they felt free to kick his scorched melon around for awhile. While Iraq may be a predominantly Islamic nation, soccer is their sport and mayhem is their World Cup. For the ebullient Guardsmen, this was a *GOOO-OO-OOOOAL!*

LTC Pingel was always ready for more things to burn, and his impatience with the fuel black market swelled as he realized that he only had a few precious months of combat command left to convince the army he should be groomed for generalship. We had been posting flyers for over a week, informing the citizenry that patronizing black market benzene suppliers helped our enemy. There was just no excuse for us to tolerate it further. It was luculently apparent to the colonel that the time for a demonstration had arrived.

It didn't take long to find someone breaking the rules. The first fuel entrepreneur the cav's command element found was selling gas on a major street, right out in front of Allah and everybody. The medicine man talked a mile a minute as a phalanx of American hoplites advanced on him, weapons at low ready. Realizing we were serious, he braced himself for a stiff lecture.

But the commander of the largest area of responsibility within 1-25 Brigade's purview wasted no words. He ordered the man flex-cuffed, blindfolded and loaded up. Customers were relieved of their purchases and chased off. GIs set about pouring each container of gasoline into the gutter to be filtered by Tall Afar's sophisticated groundwater runoff management system, otherwise known as "dirt."

Some of those present—it seems a bit too precious to refer to them as "cooler heads"—prevailed upon LTC Pingel not to set the black marketer's little van on fire. He was going to be detained anyway, and the unmonitored van would undoubtedly be stolen within the hour. It took significant persuasion, but finally the colonel assented to leaving the scene untorched.

Halfway to his Stryker, he turned on his heel.

"Damn it," he said, "these people will never learn if we just let 'em get away with it."

Yanking a thermite grenade off his vest, the God of War directed one of his air guards to break a window out of the van. Then he pulled the pin and lobbed in his grenade, and the whole damned street caught fire.

Commandos were useful, but there was always a price to pay. Brave and effective *peshmerga* Kurds, they went everywhere in country and took on any mission without a second thought. On the other hand, they cared nothing for Iraqis in general, were totally unaccountable for their actions, and absolute Hell on their brand-new, appliance-white Dodge Ram pickups (thank you, taxpayers of America).

They also consumed more resources than our co-located ING battalion. Iraqi troops on FOB Sykes were kept segregated into their own cantonment area, which was surrounded by triple-strand concertina wire, constantly supervised by U.S. advisors and guarded day and night. It would be fair to say they weren't given the full run of the place.

Whenever the commandos rolled onto the FOB they had to be separately housed, since the chances of them killing a few of their brothers in arms was fairly substantial. If you told them to kill some folks, there was a one-hundred percent chance the commandos would comply. If you didn't tell them whom to kill, they would find someone without much prodding—they didn't care much for Shiites and they flat hated Sunnis. They liked the heck out of Americans, pretty women, and anyone who spoke Kurdish to them. Even bad Kurdish.

So the commandos ended up hooched on their own special pad, one usually reserved for visiting American units that joined our resident cavalry squadron for large operations.

They were great guys who loved to eat and laugh and shoot at things. It was always interesting to join them on an op, provided you stayed out of their sector of fire, which was 360 degrees from where they stood at any given moment.

MAJ Bailey had a story he liked to tell about the *peshmerga* commander. While the ING would often disappear for weeks after they got their officer-lightened pay packets, commandos never even took leave—they were having too much fun on their jobs. They despised the lily-livered INGs and weren't shy about saying so.

Finally, we got intel that a number of our ING battalion's permanent disappearances hadn't been desertions after all.

A friendly local cabbie who was approved to hang out near the gate and take our *jundis* on their leaves had developed an unpleasant habit. He would get Iraqi soldiers in the car and drive them straight to al Sarai, where they would be dragged out of the cab and skull-shot. For this accommodation, he collected fifty bucks a head from Ali Baba.

This cabbie had been detained and seen the evidence presented against him, but our interrogators hadn't broken him. The *peshmerga* commander had a suggestion.

"You give him me. We fuck up him."

Our S-3 officer gave back a tall, easy smile and said, "We can't let you beat on the boy."

"No—we fuck him up. You give him."

"No, really," MAJ Bailey said. "That ain't the way we do it. You can't beat him."

The commando colonel was nonplussed. He looked down, thought about it, then walked over to the major's desk and pantomimed slamming the cabbie down over the blotter by his hair. Then he demonstrated huge pelvic thrusts.

"You're gonna... *fuck* the guy?"

"Yes! Up! We fuck *up* him!"

"*You* do that?," MAJ Bailey asked. "*All* y'all do that? Are you serious?"

Apparently, during his earlier Persian Gulf tour as a young tank commander, MAJ Bailey hadn't encountered this precise scenario.

"Everybody do it! Whole unit fuck up him!

"Then," and here the commando leader waggled his

eyebrows and grinned, "he talk.

"Maybe, even he will... sing?"

The commandos left about a week later, pulling out in their big white Dodge Rams, revving the engines, smoking the tires and waving furiously. They are first-rate allies, the *peshmerga*, and definitely the brawlers you want on your side in a street fight. Maybe not the guys you want dating your little brother.

It wasn't until they'd departed that SGT Tilley, the FOB "mayor," inspected their billets and realized there had been an oversight when they were in-processed. Nobody had briefed them on use of the latrines.

In true field-expedient fashion, the capable commandos had simply picked out one corner of each steel hooch and squatted there, wiping up afterward with their hands and unloading their fingers by smearing long streaks down the walls.

SGT Tilley later described those hooches as "time-out rooms in an insane asylum."

We were 300 meters past the Shoot House, a destroyed building slumping in on itself, overlooking Route Santa Fe. The Shoot House was a favorite sniper hidey hole from which to take potshots at the Americans and detonate IEDs. It had once been the police academy, until it was sacked and burned by insurgents who got medieval on its ass. The newly dominant tribe known as 2-14 Cavalry had since been over it and through it, burned it and blasted out partitions, dug through its rubble and thumped away at its outside walls with .50-cals. It had no roof and only a few straggling bits of facade remaining, but its reputation was such that we always beady-eyed it from our armored convoys when we rumbled past. One glint from within was enough to precipitate gittin' yer shoot on.

So it was that most everyone was looking left toward the Shoot House when the radio sputtered, "STOP STOP STOP—there's a mine in the road!"

The first Stryker had already been passing by it when their air guard spotted an anti-personnel mine on the right side of the road. It wasn't much of an installation, just sitting there at the edge of the road, waving its little antenna at me as I looked down at it from the right side air guard hatch before ducking inside and feeling foolish. Could it even hurt me from there? An earache, maybe a cut. That mine was designed to take the feet off a walking man, not penetrate the hull of a Stryker, but it could be wired to a bigger boom. I popped my head back out as our vehicle circled left off the road into the gritty flat in front of the Shoot House. After a quick discussion about whether or not to wait for EOD, our VC instructed his .50-cal gunner to take out the mine with single shot fire.

The M2 .50-caliber machine gun is an estimable weapon, a formidable engine of war so capable it has remained mostly unchanged from John Browning's original design for over 85 years. After destroying targets in World War II, the Korean War, Vietnam and every brushfire that marked the years between those infernos, the Ma Deuce is mounted to this day on tanks, trucks, APCs, IFVs, technicals, helos, ships, ADA quad mounts and fighter jets. The fifty-cal can even be set to single-shot mode for long-range sniping, but that doesn't work very well with its distance-adjustable leaf sight unless the gunner has doped out a detailed range card for each barrel and practiced plenty—as this gunner obviously had not.

BOOM! Two feet off. BOOM! Three feet high. The crew was laughing. In the middle distance, Iraqis scuttled into their houses. BOOM! Another miss, six feet short.

We were in defilade from the road, in case the little exposed mine triggered a big, buried IED. The mine lay about 40 meters from our position, nearly level with the top of the vehicle.

I looked at the squad leader in the air guard hatch next to me. Straphangers have need of tact. PSYOP were rarely in our own vehicle and we rode with lah-dee dah-dee everybody, so we were perpetually the new kids wherever we went. But the wiry E6 riding next to me seemed pretty alert, so I reached over and tapped him on the sleeve. He jumped a bit, looked at me, pulled an earpiece away so he could hear.

"Hey, Staff—see those houses over there?," I asked. "Ma Deuce'll go right through the walls at this range."

"So?" SSG Thorpe summed up the situation in brief. "They shouldn't've fuckin' let someone lay a mine here," he said.

That seemed a reasonable reaction from a man who had been blown up a few times and interviewed hundreds of Iraqis who never knew anything and who always professed to be teachers in schools that weren't open, but I was stuck with being the culturally sensitive PSYOP guy. Cultural sensitivity starts with minimizing civilian casualties.

"Yeah, but your gunner can't hit shit, and an M4 should take care of that little thing anyways."

He grinned a little, and thumbed the mike switch on his CVC helmet.

"Hey, gunner, knock that shit off. You couldn't hit the ground if you tripped.

"Lemme get this."

SSG Thorpe took a precision dip of Cope and pushed up out of his hatch. Laying prone across the top of the Stryker, he winked at me and said, "You might want to plug your ears. I'll get this in one.

"Now watch this."

Crack. Crack. Crack. No joy. Peering through my little dime store Coleman binos, I called out his shot placement as he slow-fired: high left, low right, low left. Thorpe stopped firing and looked at his rifle quizzically, shook it lightly as if to scare out the demons possessing it. Now his own scouts were laughing at him. That couldn't be good. Thorpe shot again. *Crack.* High right, rifle jammed.

While SSG Thorpe took immediate action to clear his weapon, I leaned my elbows on the steel roof and looked through my rifle's optic. At four-power magnification, the little mine looked like a shipping crate. I hit it once, made it jump. Hit it again, and *pop* went the weasel. No bigger booms hidden under the road.

Not that time.

SSG Thorpe gave me a sour look, but since everyone had been looking at the mine, no one knew who shot it but him and me. As he lowered his feet back down through the hatch, I pushed my thumb against the spring pressure of the CVC switch.

"Nice shooting, Sar'nt Thorpe."

They were parked by the roadside on FOB Road as we rolled out with that night's LOGPAC. Six ING trucks, four small white Toyota pickups with no armor and a cargo truck (also unarmored) big enough to carry a heavy platoon. One pickup, hood open, steamed gently into the night air. Probably was running whatever was left, if any, of the break-in oil the factory poured into it on the day it was built.

Every detail was clearly emphasized because every vehicle had all of its lights on. *Jundis* walked around smoking, talking, waving flashlights. Nobody pulled security. Everybody stayed within the warm refuge of high-intensity lighting.

Just one big, happy target.

We couldn't stop to set them straight. We had half a dozen heavy trucks, three HMMWVs and a Stryker escort, headed all the way to Mosul.

Sitting in the turret with a drive-on rag over my face, I just looked at them and shook my head. For months, I'd been patting my head and pointing at *jundis'* unworn helmets, reminding them to set up perimeters and enforcing noise and light discipline. Me, and about a hundred thousand other joes who didn't feel like getting capped because the ING or IA couldn't be persuaded to act professional for the duration of one whole mission.

Much has been made of the strategic error of failing to retain Iraqi Army commanders and troops, especially the vaunted Republican Guard, to maintain the sovereignty of a newly constituted, democratic Iraq. These would be the same Republican Guard troops that dissolved in the briefest of battles to "melt away" into the populace. Such "elite" troops now formed some fuzzily calculated percentage of the resistance, insurgency or terror campaign—depending on the definition by your favored think tank or politico—and this was constantly pointed out as a colossal policy blunder.

We damn well should have held onto those seasoned Iraqi troops. Hundreds of thousands of them, utilizing sophisticated human wave assaults and backed by the merest billions in U.S. aid, managed to battle Iran to a stalemate in only fifteen years.

They're just that good.

"We'll stand down when the Iraqi Army stands up" was the line we'd been fed, but the IA had been standing up units since we'd been in-country. In many villages, it was the only game in town for employment, so they had a tremendous recruitment rate.

Retention? Not so much. The ING battalion stationed at FOB Sykes, touted as one of their elite units, boasted a mere 55 percent desertion rate. Granted, many of them returned eventually—just not necessarily in possession of their rifles and uniforms.

Off the FOB, you could buy ING uniforms for four bucks, U.S. uniforms with nametapes for about 25 (much less than their replacement cost at Clothing Sales), and any kind of weapon that matched your martial fantasies and fell within your budget. "Melting away" these days meant ditty-bopping down to the black market for some extra cash.

We would find those uniforms later when we boomed a door open to toss a house, and we would reclaim them as evidence, detaining their new owners for indefinite periods before usually releasing them uncharged. Later, the same uniforms would be re-issued to the Iraqi National Guard, who would desert in vast percentages and re-sell those uniforms in the Great Circle of Death.

It was a bloody strange economic model, but it did accelerate the dollar.

As we drove by the show-lit shooting gallery on FOB Road that night, I decided I couldn't care less. It wasn't my turn to baby-sit *jundis* anymore. Let the next guy stand them up, stand them down, waltz them around. This was our last convoy, headed back to FOB Freedom to rejoin our detachment, pack up and fly home. Along the way, I would be offered many chances to reenlist.

Thinking of that, I smiled under my dust rag. Old soldiers would never die.

We'd just melt away.

IN THE BIN

'Tis true, 'tis certain; man though dead retains
Part of himself: the immortal mind remains.

—Homer, *The Iliad*

Three days after I de-planed at SeaTac and rode home to peel off sticky, faded desert camo for the last time, I was dispatched by my exotically sexy wife to attend to her mother in the mental ward.

In Texas.

With barely a hug and certainly no kisses under our belts, it seemed early in the reacquaintance process to be leaving the state. Mine not to question why; mine but to salute and execute.

Does that ever go away, that reflex to saddle up and follow orders? My outcomes from it hadn't generally been optimal, but the key in my back never seemed to fall out no matter how hard I danced The Chicken to shake it loose.

Down in Houston, my sister-in-law had broken into Hu Ma-Ma's house. After calling several times, Lin had scaled the garden gate and peered through the sliding glass door to find her mother bleeding out onto the kitchen floor.

Taking a firm grip on the red oak grip of her Japanese vegetable cleaver, Ma had sliced her radial veins wide open at the elbow where their torn edges twitched in trauma, sluicing out her blood fast enough to rapidly depress her brain-bruising blood pressure of 185/123.

She wasn't messing around.

So I spent a few days at the hospital there. Melanie didn't come along, and I never questioned her about that. The Yellow Rose of Seattle had work to do—responsible corporate work, not puttering around the aisles of a dusty old hardware store, or scribbling notes about a so-called war that nobody cared about. There were markets to build, currencies to trade, the Nisei to track, credit defaults to swap around.

Anyway, it has to be hard, thinking of your own mother that despondent, so I bit my lip and succeeded—at the expense of badly tattered lip linings—not to remind my sleek wife that we never visited my own mother, one state away in Oregon, because lovely Melanie insisted that visiting my family stressed her out.

Besides, her Ma and I always got along pretty well—at least after that first visit. That was the time that Ma and her one daughter, two sons and squealing grandson visited our new home in one cackling group, not three months into our marriage.

Clothing was immediately strung all over the house on Mel's older brother's insistence that his shirts had to be air-dried, indoors. We did four loads of dishes every day, countless laundry (much of it snot-encrusted toddler duds), and later received a

$387.00 water bill in an envelope containing an advisory from the Lake Forest Park Water District to investigate for plumbing leaks.

Silent as a Guatemalan domestic, I chauffeured the gibbering clan around the Northwest in my four wheel-drive, club cab company truck. We toured from Mount Rainier to the Space Needle to Stevens Pass, where my erstwhile nephew shrieked his outrage and hunched rigidly into a fetal position after we'd paid up front for his ski rental and a private lesson. At the next pay period, I reimbursed my company for $636.00 of gasoline charges without even attempting an explanation.

Three days into this family bonding gala, Mel decided she'd had enough. She left the building.

Realizing that I no longer spoke the native language of my house (press "one" for Mandarin, "two" for Taiwanese), I sought refuge in the garage, first carving a wooden spoon for Ma, then pounding away with a thick rawhide mallet to chop out dovetails for a set of pine book boxes Melanie had requested. Maybe they would come right. Maybe they would make her happy. Maybe she wouldn't just... well, leave.

Poking her head out the door, Ma frowned and told me I was making too much noise, so I grabbed a book and went back in to sit quietly on the sofa, grimly fixated on the anticipated relief of getting up early and bolting for a job site in Lewis County, 96 miles to the south.

The Chinese can narrow their eyes very effectively, leaving nothing but a black hole to nowhere as you fall into a rabbit hole of bottomless, angry pupils. Sitting on the love seat across from me, Ma pinned me with a basilisk stare evidently inherited from her daughter.

"So," she said, arching her eyebrows, "this happen…often?"

The woman had personally experienced the fall of Chiang Kai-Shek and later gathered her family to flee Nicaragua as refugees. I couldn't bullshit Ma. I closed the paperback and spread my hands, palms up.

"Ma, I don't even know where she is. This is all new to me."

"You have temper, too. Sometime, not only what you say. Sometime how you look.

"You give The Face."

"*Hunh…* ?" This was a piece of cultural awareness of which I had remained innocent. "What's 'The Face'?"

Ma shoved out her bottom lip. She scowled like a temple gargoyle and growled like a riled Pekingese dog, and I couldn't help myself. For the first time since that locust swarm descended on our house to criticize Melanie's cooking and snicker at the bumbling American, I laughed. I kept laughing until I was snuffling snot and blinking hot salt water, and then I looked at her presentation of The Face again, and bent over holding my gut and laughed some more.

Mel had gone and left me to her befuddled family and I was an ogre and Ma was modeling The Face like a Chinese opera fright mask and it was the best, funniest joke ever, or at least the best all day.

Ma's eyes got big. She pulled her head back like a startled cat, cocked it over to the side and looked at me funny until finally she laughed, too. I wanted to hug her then, but I hadn't earned it yet.

So we went into the light-filled kitchen of that low-mileage house and I cut up fruit while Ma figured out the cupboard plan and found some pots and staples and spices ("Why you no have... what you call it?"), and we fed everyone into caloric oblivion until Melanie returned the next evening, hard-eyed and silent, and the honeymoon with her family was over. It was a couple of years before I got up the nerve to ask her where she went that day.

And night.

My jet-setting, sleek corporate wife chuckled expansively then, answering that she'd driven on up to Canada to spend the night at a hotel. She gave me to know it was my fault, as if there had ever been any doubt of that. There were no further details offered and given her snarling, hair-trigger jealousy, I didn't think to ask.

I never do. Probably I don't learn much that way. Maybe I don't want to know much.

Maybe I already know more than I want to.

Ma and I achieved some understanding after that day. She didn't speak English comfortably and I had about five words of Chinese that I could recognize in Seattle and maybe a hundred when immersed in Houston's Chinese community, but it was hardly an obstacle. We saw eye to eye on the bigger issues.

For the next few years, I habitually toted a sack of tools south when we visited Ma so I could kick-start the balky attic furnace, patch the roof, replace her hot water heater or just screw in a few light bulbs that had gone untended since her husband was laid out in state at the hospice, desiccated like a Pringle but still pulling breath while my wife moistened his lips with a soft cloth and her older sister enforced round after round of chanting, bejeweled, Buddhist ritual prayer.

I prayed for him to go ahead and die. By that point cancer and chemo had combined to immolate his body away like a soft wax candle, leaving Mr. Hu looking like a concentration camp internee who escaped by shambling blindly through the roaring ovens.

Because Ma was a wheel in the Chinese community there, ensconced into a weekly educational TV gig and beloved of Houston's successive mayoralties, her husband's demise would by necessity conjure a veritable pageant of squawking horns, flowing red silk banners and gilded dragons. After that, it fell to me to fix up the house.

What else was I going to do? I was *gwai loh*, Big Nose, Foreign Devil, Round Eye. I was the honky edition of "Guess Who's Coming to Dinner?" Friends of the family would come to stare when I was visiting, check me out from the corners of their epicanthic eyes and chatter cheerfully in front of my back. I could either sit there, vacantly staring at the big screen and pretending they were talking sports, or get up and grab a hammer.

But I could fix up her decaying Eighties tract house, and Ma could fix supper like nobody's business, and—pale hair or not—it wasn't like she was likely to have another son-in-law to cook for anytime soon. My sister-in-law was firmly betrothed to the seven incontinent rescue dogs fenced off into the various stench-pillowed corners of her tiny condo. There would never be a dowry big enough for Lin, but at least we built her a fence on one of our in-law shuttle diplomacy junkets. Then Ma cooked me one of her dinners that couldn't be beat.

"She never cooks like that for anyone else," my wife said with a strange little smile. "I guess you must rate."

Then my sweet little thang strode back into the living room to dive into another screaming battle in Mandarin, and I went back to hoovering my plate. Eventually—per routine and in the interest of securing the shredded remains of domestic tranquility—I dragged her gently out, grabbed our stuff from the guest room and threw it into a cab to head for the Red Lion Inn.

That was back in the sane times.

That was before I trotted off to war, or put a nine-millimeter to my skull just to feel the brain-cooling muzzle steel as I eased on pressure, flirting with the gentle break of my Glock's trigger safety as relief rushed toward me out of the darkness like a midnight train; before Ma was committed for her own protection; before Melanie went to a Wyoming spread to spend Thanksgiving with a boyfriend whose name I never learned and never will. One might even call them the good times, if one hadn't seen better.

I wasn't allowed to talk to the doctors.

Mel's sister Lin took care of that, bustling officiously around the nuthatch when she wasn't demanding provisioning runs to PetSmart in my M&M-shaped rental car. I stood there, hands behind my back; physically hard, mentally vacant, waiting for further instructions. Doctors and nurses and orderlies provided plenty of those.

"What does she need, Doc?" *How high?*

"She needs to get up and walk, as much as possible. She can't just sit on her bed all day." *You better GIT yo' raggedy ass in GEAR, soldier! Move! MOVE!*

Ma didn't want to get up. She didn't want to put on her slippers. She complained that her bandages were too tight, tried to unwrap each bruised, lacerated arm with the opposite steel-cloven extremity. She was dizzy. With frail determination, she pushed away her meds.

On a break outside in the sweaty Houston sunshine, I called my Mom.

"I don't even know what I'm doing here."

"Why isn't Melanie there?"

"She has to work."

"Don't you think you should be taking care of your... wife?"

"Jesus, I don't know. I canceled my appointments with Björn."

"Your VA counselor?"

"Yeah. And I missed a visit with Malia."

"Jack, you need to take care of yourself first."

"I'm okay!"

"Sure you are." Mom paused a moment. "Then your daughter. Then your wife. Then other people."

"Yeah, you're a perfect example."

She laughed a little, and sighed. "You can't be a doormat."

I cleared my throat. Mom laughed again, only just a little, and said, "Very funny.

"Tell her you love her, then go home, Jack.

"Go home."

"I don't even know where that is, Mom.

"Love you bunches."

"I love you, too, dear. Do what you need to do, then go home.

"Promise me."

"Bye, Mom. Love you."

What I needed to do, according to the doctors, was get that trooper moving. It was time to be a sergeant again.

So up I went to the tenth floor, back through the triple security doors where they checked my ID just as if I hadn't been there twice a day for the past three days, and zagged left down the hall to Ma's room.

She shared quarters with a fat, grey-blonde woman who sat on the back bunk, too despondent to knot her pink terry bathrobe closed over the juddering, blue-veined colossi cascading sloppily over her cask-shaped belly. Whenever I walked into their room, she would squint intently at me from within the petulant folds of her purple-skinned face until I glanced her way, then dramatically flounce her robe together, clearly offended by my insolent invasion of her ladylike privacy.

There are few enough amusements in the booby hatch, I suppose.

Ma, for her part, huddled over in the corner, practicing escape and evasion tactics to avoid the spoon zeroing in on her mouth. I took over from the orderly and Ma looked at me gratefully until she realized that I, too, would try to feed her.

"C'mon, Ma. This stuff's better than what KBR fed us."

"I don't like. My cooking better. Miss my own cooking."

"Me, too, Ma. Me, too. So how about you eat some of this... uh, whatever it is... and then we'll take a walk, and pretty soon we'll get you home so you can make a big pot of beef noodle soup."

She looked at me and the glaze came off her eyes for a moment. "You li'e my beef noodle."

"Yeah, Ma. I sure do."

The overcast grayed out her eyes again, and she looked down through the floor. From where she sat, I was pretty sure she could see all the way to Hell.

"I hate this place. Hate my life." She looked at me with something like the opposite of The Face. "Hate everything."

"Ma, don't say that." *Who're you fuckin' kidding, HE-ro?*

"Where is Mei Li?"

"I told you before, Ma, remember? Melanie couldn't come this time."

"Where *Hu Mei-Li?!*"

"Ah, Ma, you know she'll come through. We have to trust her, huh?"

I stroked her hair, waiting for the meds to kick in so I could feed her a little.

After a few bites of something like mashed pears, Ma started averting her head with birdlike quickness. By the time I had to dab her face with a cloth after each near-miss, we were ready to take our little walk.

When I slipped fuzzy bunnies over her swollen feet, Ma gave me The Face with an exponent and feebly kicked me in the eye. I couldn't blame her for that—it wasn't the Middle East; she didn't mean anything by it—so I ignored her toe shot and put one hand on her closest biceps, well above the tattered elbow, and wrapped my other arm gently around her shoulders.

Ma and I carefully stepped out to pad up and down the main hallway, very slowly and nowhere near the secured, alarmed triple doors. According to our pattern, we would continue until she got too testy and desperate to continue our little march.

There was a lean, muscled young man on that ward. Once set in motion (*yes, Drill Sergeant!*), he shuffled unaided up and down our shared venue, regular as a metronome, never pausing or questioning his routine.

While Ma leaned on my elbow, the lad leaned on the adjustable steel tubing of the IV stand that was steadily dripping balance back into his life. With a white-knuckled grip from his big, red fist, he battened onto that stand like it was a wheeled shepherd's crook.

Slowly, he advanced his left foot, then hesitantly brought the right foot even, then repeated the process. With painful deliberation, looking neither left nor right (*if you needed peripheral vision, we'd've ISSUED you some*), he measured out his testudineous cadence hour after lonely hour. High blood pressure and elbow bandages be damned, my 78 year-old mother-in-law was flat kicking his ass in these little wind sprints.

He consistently stepped out first with his left foot. That's a military march habit, so I looked again and saw him. Despite his vacant stare, he wore his cornflower-embellished, butt-crack hospital gown with regimental posture. His brushy blonde hair was trimmed flat on the top, shaved high and tight up the sides.

There wasn't enough gown fabric to cover his arms, peculiarly hypertrophic in the instantly recognizable fashion of those who have performed way too many pushups. Still vibrantly saturated and crisply lined, the bullet-torn flag coloring his thick biceps hadn't flown there long. I wondered which post town had supplied the artist: Fayetteville, North Carolina? Tillicum, Washington? Killeen, Texas?

I wondered where he'd lost it, gone off the reservation, disconnected himself from the unthinkable by some unthinkable act: Fallujah in al Anbar, Iraq? Bagram, Afghanistan? Killeen, Texas...?

All through the darkening hours after Ma went on strike from walking to sit disconsolate on her bed, that soldier pushed his IV rack up and down the sodium-lit, gray-waxed, speckled tiles of the loony bin hallway. *Yo' lef', yo' lef', yo' lef'-right-LEYUF!*

Sitting in the plastic chair just inside Ma's door, I wondered who to call next. I wondered when my flight left, and where it would land.

Dressed in split-hide desert boots and a Calloway golf shirt, I sat there for a long time and listened to his IV stand squeak up and down, up and down, up and down. The squeak got louder each time he approached her door, then diminished in a predictable, slo-mo Doppler fade as he passed, the wobbling chrome support giving him one last, tangible thing to hold onto in the night.

Wondering who would come for him, who would saddle up and make the time and prove to all of us that no soldier will be left behind, I went and stood in the door. I watched him walk past, one dragging step at a time, and as he came even with the door I stood to attention and saluted him, never making eye contact, looking straight ahead. He never broke stride, or glanced sideways into that sad little room. He kept going straight on into the night.

But three slow steps past the door, the broken soldier halted. The dirge-paced squeaking stopped for the first time that day. Soundlessly, without turning around, he took his big, sunburned hand off that IV stand and raised it up in a small wave.

I wanted nothing more than for someone to hug him but it couldn't be me, so I turned toward the ward doors (*column right, MARCH!*) and left the hospital (*double time, MARCH!*) and rushed on and on, straight into the night and free, maybe, going home or anyway somewhere.

A LITTLE BIT RUSTY

I returned, and saw under the sun, that the race [is] not to the swift, nor the battle to the strong, neither yet bread to the wise, nor yet riches to men of understanding, nor yet favour to men of skill; but time and chance happeneth to them all.

—Ecclesiastes 9:11

I threw myself into Operation Peacetime with a will. Articles were written and submitted, applications filled out for state and city positions.

With money that Mel had saved out of my deployment pay, I rented shop space from a hardware store acquaintance in Ballard, a maritime industrial neighborhood of Seattle slowly gentrifying away from its lutefisk-soaked roots, and bought a big, green General mortiser to speed up furniture construction.

Despite its no longer convenient location, I rejoined my little gym in the U-District. Brown and green bottles piled up in the recycling tote. Hardwick's took me back in on a part-time basis, opening up for two hours in the morning. I would get to building a boat soon, after I had a customer base built up.

Claiming a vintage BMW motorcycle from my step-dad, I took a head-clearing ride to visit my brother in Idaho.

Rich with detail, life was accelerating.

One day I got up and went to the front door. My plans were to hit the gym, go to the shop and meet Will later for a beer and some catching up, until it occurred to me rather suddenly that the very last thing I wanted to do was go out that door.

I put my hand on the doorknob. Then I took my hand off the knob. Outside, our neighborhood was typically quiet. "It's quiet—*too* quiet" is the way a hack screenwriter might have dialogued it.

"Well, I'll just go back upstairs for a few minutes, knock out some stuff on the computer, and head out after that."

I told myself, "I'm in no hurry."

Since I wasn't convincing myself, I called my wife at work in Tacoma and whined down the phone line at her.

"It's okay, sweetie," she said. "Just do what you need to do.

"I think you're doing great."

"I'm doing *nothing*."

"You're doing all kinds of things! You started a business, and took a motorcycle trip, and had a visit with Malia, and..."

"Sweets, I *really* don't want to go outside. It's weird. I never had this feeling before."

"So don't. Why do you have to?"

"I promised Will."

"Call him up. He'll understand."

"I don't think so." Actually, I was a little afraid that he *would* understand: I was freaked out, scared to leave the house.

By definition, sergeants are not afraid. I took Will to Iraq, from which he came home with a Purple Heart while I was untouched. I was his sergeant. Sergeants lead from the front. Ergo, I could not be afraid.

Twenty-five minutes before I was due to meet Will, I charged out the door and jumped into my truck, lurching into the starting ritual (five pumps, lots of choke, step on the foot starter while reducing choke until she lights, push choke most of the way in, move foot to gas pedal and catch her before she dies, adjust the set throttle to high idle for two minutes) before I could decide not to go.

I made it there on time, Will and I shared a pitcher or two, and I left the bar without my credit card.

That was the first time. There were a lot more times after that.

The carpets were a fabulous, desert-toned cartography of wrinkle-edged urine stains, topographically enhanced by crusted mounds of sputum, hairball, vomit and dingle berries plastered with shiny fur mats.

All of the furniture I built for Melanie had been abused by piss and claw, including our solid cherry eating table, cedar-lined blanket chest of maple and African rosewood, and the sofa table made from a hand-selected slab of swirl-grain Haitian Raintree accented with chocolate-dark Peruvian walnut edging. Out in the garage, the tools I used to build those things—my restored 1946 Walker Turner bandsaw, 15-inch Jet planer and even the three-horsepower, 220-volt tablesaw I bought with my grandfather's bequest—were pitted with the rust of a thousand strafing runs by furry tail gunners.

I stared at them for awhile, and wondered if I remembered how to cry.

But I could build it all again, strap it back together. I could put all of it right and make it solid.

I had the tools.

Melanie never bought my excuses.

"Are you going in to your shop today?," she would ask. "That's your blood money you're spending on rent."

Blood money. When she said things like that, I would remind myself that English was her third language, after Mandarin Chinese and Nicaraguan Spanish.

"My back's still hurting," I would say. Or, "Gimme a couple of days to strap this manuscript together, then I can mail it off to somebody and quit thinking about it forever."

You can't hide fear under words, or excuse it by discomfort.

The day the dream of my shop turned into a nightmare came right out of the wild blue. I had done a couple of small jobs, chair repairs and a simple little end table, and was sinking my carbide teeth into an exotic dining table project to be built of African *wenge* with contrasting white ash trim.

There I stood, finally in business for myself, busily beating my assault rifle into bandsaw blades. Looking up from sketching, I surveyed my demesnes: a swathe of beloved tools, from my tiny brass finger plane to the mighty Unisaw, surrounded me in patterns carefully orchestrated for workflow, tidiness and organization. Custom electrical cordage fired my 220-volt machinery, which was all connected to a metal-ducted dust collection system. Japanese, German and New Hampshirean hand saws hung over my custom seven-foot workbench. Over the back alley loading dock, I could see the dry-docks and fishermen's boatyards of Old Ballard.

Peace in our time.

I was wholly unprepared for the 24-foot walls to rush madly in at me. The whole picture tilted and slid sideways into Fear. I knew the pigeons in the high eaves weren't snipers, but I ducked behind my bench anyway. When I felt my hands start to shake, I held them up in front of my face and couldn't recognize them.

Somebody was whimpering, and that's a thing I don't do, but no one else was in the building. Chastising myself for a weak-kneed crybaby, I took two deep breaths, pushed myself up and picked up a micro-sharpened pencil to finish my detail drawing.

I stared at the drawing without the least understanding. Nothing on the page was intelligible. Incomprehensible as hieroglyphics to a dog, the sketch swam in front of me and the most taboo thought, the sure knowledge that I had held at bay throughout a whole tour where I felt like a fraud, an old broke-dick hack masquerading as a soldier and a leader, exploded into my head.

I can't do this.

"Sure you can," I told myself, sergeant to my own cowering private. "You built all your own furniture, and some for other people. Some of it's even pretty cool."

Oh, yeah?, said the smart-assed private. *How?*
If you're so smart, tell me how I did that.

To reassure him, I conjured up the memory of a blanket chest I built for our master bedroom. It was a frame-and-panel maple carcase with polished copper sheathing over aromatic cedar panels. The lid featured a glorious wide panel of *bubinga*, also known as African rosewood. It was a complex, well-executed, beautiful piece. I smiled, visualizing it, until my stomach dropped away with the realization that I had absolutely no idea how I'd built it.

In the bottom of my rollaway tool chest lay a Glock 19 with a rail-mounted tactical light. I kept it locked away there, snuggled into a black, trouser-clip holster five miles from home, so that it wouldn't be anywhere close to me at night.

But just then I pulled it out and held it in a two-handed combat grip, dropping the magazine and cycling the action, until it became obvious that out of a shopful of solid equipment, my pistol was the only tool I felt competent to use.

That's when the Fear moved in, asserting that its rent was paid years and years ahead.

By September 2005, I'd achieved the sort of steady drinking rhythm that was so comfortable as to be unnoticeable.

Before I deployed, I had established a pace, over the course of six or seven years, of maybe ten beers in the summertime. Those were mostly occasional microbrews with Dale in the corner house and a *cerveza* or two when our Mexican neighbors, with whom we shared a sprawling filbert tree, threw one of their famous bull roasts. Scotch is the best drink for winter (Ardbeg was my poisonal preference) and I typically would sip my way through most of a liter over the course of one of our gray north-wet winters. Mornings, I would have my cup of coffee.

In September, I walked out to take our recycling to the curb, and the small of my back strained when I lifted the glass tote. Peering into it, I discovered dozens of beer bottles and three (three!) empty scotch liters. Winter hadn't even started yet.

By this point, I had deferred to wiser friends and started talking to Björn, a VA counselor who actually knew WTF he was talking about. Björn's calm observation on the booze was that I should slow down. Failing that, he had a group in mind that I might want to attend, and I had a fair idea which group it was. Since I do not like groups and was going broke anyway, I quit buying beer forthwith. It would take a little while to get through the leftovers, though—not to mention the cupboard full of scotch.

There was always coffee, anyway. A couple pots a day kept the doctor at bay. By the time I got wound into usefulness at eleven or so, it was time to start thinking about lunch. A nice coffee after lunch made facing work seem more realistic. I usually didn't have much after-dinner coffee.

Two or three cups, maximum.

SILHOUETTE

Every man is as Heaven made him, and sometimes a great deal worse.

–Miguel de Cervantes,
The Ingenious Gentleman Don Quixote of La Mancha

I quickly learned to hate recycling day. Before I left, the bottle tote—glass tote, actually, but how many jars of spaghetti sauce can you go through in two weeks?—was never full. Not half-full, either, or even a quarter.

"How much do you drink?," was a question asked of me many times by many departments. Before I left, there had been a battery of physical and mental exams. It turned out my government cared to know quite a bit about me, in order that I might serve it better. After I returned, there were counseling sessions, more physicals, and a raft of lectures on self-preservation in the new, dangerous world of peace at home. They told me not to take it too fast, not to drink too much, and not to beat my wife.

"Thank you for your service" is what people say to your face while they're secretly analyzing you to see if you'll go off unexpectedly, like a flash-bang grenade when some newbie forgot to tape down the spoon.

Suddenly the VA wanted to know on a detailed, week-by-week basis how much I drank. "Enough to go to sleep on," or "two or three with dinner" was not getting it for them.

They wanted accuracy and repeatability, like zeroing a weapon. Hard to zero when you can't focus. Hard to focus when you can't sleep. Hard to sleep when you pass out first. Even harder after two pots of coffee to crank my cold-diesel head in the morning.

The answer used to be less than one bottle of beer a week, good northwest micro-brews or nothing. Maybe the odd shot of Ardbeg single malt whisky on a cold winter evening. Now I was clocking more than a tote per week of cheap six-packs, but that's as close as I cared to count. So the bottles stacked up. Sometimes, I carried them out and hid them in the garage, behind my pile of dusty rucksacks and motorcycle inner tubes, next to the smashed rocking chair I promised Mom I would rebuild. It will never be the same, though.

"Jack, did you get the garbage and recycling out?"

"Yeah, got it, sweetie!," I'd call back, rattling the bottles for effect and silently stashing them behind an old chunk of oily plywood leaning up against the side wall of the garage. No way could I give that many booze bottles to the garbage man.

I wasn't ready for that.

But I was ready for Sunday. Chore day. A day of planned activities that Mel and I would do together. I wouldn't have to leave the house alone. There were joint missions to perform.

In her car, we went off on our chore rotation. Along the way, we talked and held hands. I drove, dodging potholes and changing lanes to miss plastic bags. She loved me; told me so. I wondered about that, as men do.

Melanie rattled on about her boss, a former friend who had turned into a passive-aggressive abuser of subordinates. I nodded sympathetically, then forgot that I wasn't supposed to offer commentary.

"Christ," I said, watching the hands and eyes of a pedestrian in the crosswalk, "that would piss me off to no end."

Melanie looked at me, and said flatly, "Yeah."

"Everything pisses you off these days."

I pulled overwatch while she fed her feral cat colony down in the International District. It used to be called Seattle's Chinatown, but I think there may have been an ordinance passed prohibiting explicit references to ethnicity. Probably right after one of our fair city council's foreign policy resolutions.

Crouched on a rock escarpment, scanning rooftops and windows and avenues of approach, I basked in the reflected edge of her ardor for this task. She knew I didn't like cats the way she does—very few do, and they are generally called Crazy Cat Ladies. Still, we were in this thing together, bound in wedlock and sharing an adventure related to her truest passion.

Alley cats, big-eyed with avarice, pressed close, then skittered off and circled at a safe distance, yowling and rubbing on the fence. They reminded me of kids yelling for candy.

"*Moussasa*, mistah! Mistah, *moussasa!*"

"You gimme dolla, mistah!"

"Mistah, mistah, gimme you watch!"

The littlest ones had the biggest eyes, and were humbler.

"Pain seal?"

We gave out pencils until a forty-pound *jihadi* stabbed Martinez in the thigh with one, a hard overhand stroke that left him tattooed with a graphite reminder. I pushed them all out of my mind, and scanned my lane.

"Thank you for coming with me," Melanie said. Her eyes were shining, but she didn't need anything from me.

Still squatting on the rocks, I half-turned and smiled back at her. "It's one for the good guys."

"Admit it—you *love* the kitties."

Damn, she was cute. Her pony tail spilled out the back of an old Bosch Power Tools baseball cap, and she moved over the rocks the way summer waterfalls pour, spare but fluid. I felt her beauty like a fresh wound, and I knew she knew it.

"Not so much," I said. "But I'm on your side."

Operation Kitty Refreshment complete, we peeled off our rubber surgical gloves, slammed her Explorer's hatchback shut and drove to the supermarket.

The caffeine was kicking in now. Things were falling into place.

I strode into Albertson's like a man, swinging my arms in a meaningful way. I made eye contact at will. Hat in place, I'd shaved barely three days back. It was all under control. I winced when a tuft of body hair snagged in my jeans and yanked sharply at the skin of my underbelly, but tomorrow I was going to start running again, do some calisthenics, maybe even go to the little gym that was dunning me twenty-five bucks a month for nothing. Get everything back in shape. Stop looking like a slack-ass, do-nothing civilian.

The grocery aisle partitions were only six or seven feet high. The produce section, where Melanie was headed, had no cover above waist level. The place was a public riot of color. Noise came from everywhere, humming and musical and white and mechanical and conversational. I didn't listen for the words, just for tone. You can predict people from any culture by their tone, gesture, rhythm and smell. Dogs do it all the time, and they're not even the top predator.

There were too many people in the store. I tried to slow my heart, but my ears were pounding like dropping sacks of grain. My right ear beat arrhythmically, alternately fast and slow and so hard it hurt the small bones low in my head. Doctors tell me it's my heart beat, like they think I don't know how to take a pulse.

Like they think I'm over-sensitive.

A bearded guy hit on my wife over the frozen chickens and my concentration locked in, chilly-focused. Overwatching reflexively, I ratcheted up my situational awareness and stood with my hands loose from the cart handle, twelve feet off and concentrating not on her, but on the threat. I watched the Beard's eyes and hands, scanned for anyone who might be working with the guy. It was absurd and I knew it was absurd, but I automatically held my knees loose, ready to move.

If I had become some sort of jumpy gunsel and the switch couldn't be unflipped, was that a new lobe of my character, or inescapable depravity? Gain or loss? I watched everyone who approached, looked at their hands and eyes and sized them up, smiling false apology afterward.

Melanie smiled at her new friend, broke contact, looked around and took in my oversized pupils.

"What?"

"Nothing," I tried. "Sweets, can we go now? I'm not having such a good day."

"Oh, are you jealous? That man just wanted to ask me for a recipe."

"Yeah." I smiled the watery grin of a shit-eating dog. "I... sure.

"That must be it. Are you ready to check out?"

She frowned at me, worried and irritable as somebody's mother. "Do you need to go sit in the car?"

"I can finish this without you." And she would, soon enough, finish without me. Happy endings weren't out of the question.

"No, I'm okay."

"Are you sure? You don't—"

"I'm *okay*." I went and sweated over by the tall wine shelves while she finished up sorting through the meats. Towers of wine made the only decent cover in the land of plenty.

By the time we checked out, I was shaking again. I forgot the doughnut box that the cheerful, chubby, soul-patched clerk had set aside for the top of the cart and rushed out the door, chasing the rattling cart. When we discovered its lack back at home, I would feel guilty for failing that baseline task of every NCO: accountability.

Was I becoming a "type," half a step removed from mumbling in my box under a freeway overpass?

God, I was exhausted—exhausted by people, by imitating the normative social behavior I had forgotten how to parse. My hometown felt like a foreign language immersion course. I spent my time watching others closely while pretending to relax, telling myself all the while *it's safe, you idiot!*

This was what we had wanted, worked toward, waited for—even fought for: the safety of home. Why the switch wouldn't unflip, why I couldn't unring my relentless Pavlovian dingaling, were questions I couldn't answer for myself, much less for my wife who was impatient to move on.

I was never wounded. I had no excuse to huddle behind naked winter trees by the grey field stones of a downtown church, to storm out into rainy nights and hunch along head down, eyes up, keeping to the shadows.

Becoming a malingerer in my own mind put me on course to slap my own face, Patton-style, again and again until it was numb. I was unable to forgive myself for the thing I didn't know I had become.

There was no cover whatsoever out in the parking lot, filled with moving variables. The multicolored apartment building across the street was new, built with lots of windows, revetted with hide positions along the roof edge.

They all just walk around like there's nothing, I thought, they have no idea.

"What?," she said.

"I—"

I stared at her, blank. "Nothing, sweetheart."

Shit. Thinking out loud was *not* cool. Hermetically sealing my internal dialogue was the standard I set for myself. Of course, not thinking at all was the real goal. Can't give yourself enough time to think, to feel.

To fear.

Reflexively, I turned my head to the left and spat.

She grimaced. "God, I wish you wouldn't do that."

"Do what?"

"Dribble all over the place. It's disgusting. You look... *Chinese* or something."

Melanie could be pretty hard on her people. You should have heard her go off on slow-reacting Asian drivers.

"Sorry." I wasn't a spitter when I left, or a smoker, or much of a drinker, for that matter, but time flows along. We paddle downstream with whatever strokes we pick up along the way.

We all spat, everyone on the team, all the time. Partly because cigarettes make you spit (and also shit pale, poisonous liquid like a terrified dog when you sucked down your smokes with coffee in place of breakfast chow), but mostly because the greasy stink of the place—unwashed *hajjis* smelling like pit-smoked ass and the bitter dust of desiccated sewage and rich black curls of burning fuel oil—lined our throats with the rancid fur of a half-swallowed rat.

You could taste it in your snot for weeks after demobilizing, and you could never spit enough, never spit it all out if you expectorated the last drop of moisture from your body.

Without answering her, I reached for the grocery bags with my once-competent hands. Looking at the mitts on the ends of my arms, I noted that they were still knobby, hairy, familiar-looking and powerful, but my hands were strangers to me now.

Every time I looked at the furniture in our house, with hand-chiseled mortise-and-tenon frames surrounding raised panels, joined at the case corners with hand-sawn dovetails, I wondered how I had done that.

The next day the walls of my shop rushed in at me, and with a roaring head and shaking hands, I fumbled my way to a pre-programmed number for Björn, my counselor at the American Lake VA Hospital. My hands weren't even good for dialing, that day.

It seemed important to keep moving my hands. They were stiffer now that I'd broken them a couple of times, stabbed, burned, poked, folded-spindled-mutilated them, banged them on this and that. At least my fingernails weren't yellow and oiled with a nicotine stink anymore, although I missed that a lot some days. My hands were strong. There was redemption in my hands, if I could find it there again.

It was important to move my hands because when my hands thought for me and talked for me my life felt under control. I held my future in them the way I had held his team's lives in them. Like sharks, humans are really only alive when we're moving, but I had lately found it was damned hard to get out the door and get moving some days, hands or no hands.

There had been a day that I called Mel at work to announce that I didn't want to go outside. I'd been recovering from a strained back, ducking my own unaccountably terrifying woodshop until I could move my feet again without shooting burning pain into my legs.

"That's okay," she said. "Stay home and work on the computer."

"I don't think I'm explaining this right," I said. "I really don't want to go through that door.

"Like, ever."

So, hands or no hands. Because you can always drop something, can't you? A whole life can drop away through your fingers if you don't concentrate. One second of inattention and someone quits treading water in that fast river of time, goes down for good and you can build a cairn on the riverbank and cover it with ribbons and all the artifice of official glory but that's it and there it is: that guy's never coming back. No one can pull him back, no matter how strong their hands.

Will left Bothell with two strong hands, clumsy but capable in his determination. That night, I assured his dad that he would come back just the way he left, but Will came home with 7.62mm stigmata in his left hand.

What a boob I was, to think any of us would come back the way we left.

Old sergeants like to recite, "Right way, wrong way… *army* way." A kid who'd almost been recycled through Basic Training because he just couldn't seem to do anything the army way—couldn't shine his boots, shoot straight or even set up his wall locker correctly—Will came to me as a castoff from another team where SSG Caruthers had already recommended him for grade reduction at Conrad's behest.

"I don't care what your history is with Corporal Conrad," I told Will when we met. "You work for me now. Do what I need you to do, and I'll back you all the way.

"When you fuck up, it makes *me* look bad, and I don't like to look bad, so let's get our heads together on this.

"I'm going to treat you like a man, and you're going to act like one."

Hands behind his back at parade rest, Will looked down at his boots. I wondered if he noticed they needed shining. Then he looked straight back at me. There was no giving up in his expression, but there was no rebellion either. Just a willingness to try.

"Roger, Sergeant."

Not that I had any great confidence. Will did an assload of pushups while we worked things out in those first few weeks, but he started to pick up martial skills. He was a loose-footed mess of a garrison soldier who couldn't stand formality—just another part-time bonus baby, in it for the college money—but Will played the game enough to keep it out of the way of his training.

When we landed in-country, the whole detachment discovered that Will was never a garrison soldier at all. He was a warrior, and no one was more surprised to find that out than he was. I had pictured myself too old to be surprised, but after patrolling with Will Mandeville from al Anbar north to Dohuk, from Mosul to the Syrian frontier, I was surprised to find I trusted no one more. Then the bastards shot him, and I watched him fly away on a MEDEVAC bird, standing alone by the dustoff pad without anyone left to give me a hand.

Pulling into our driveway, I punched the garage door remote—a Genie, which seemed a crappy joke to me. If I ever chanced to rub a magic lamp, my first wish would have been never to see a *djinn* or the place it was from or the people who dreamed it up, ever again. My second wish would have been that no one else would have to, either. I guessed that didn't make much sense, but what did?

Grabbing our wide-based Little Giant stepladder out of the garage, I set it up at the gutter's edge.

"I need to go up on the roof while it's not raining," I told her. Also, while I wasn't shaking, but there was no need to mention that.

There was moss on the shingles, muck in the gutters. Melanie had been at me about it for a couple of weeks, but now she was being a woman again.

"Do you have to do that *now?*" She was whining in her warning tone of control: do it my way or it'll get ugly. "I thought we were going to spend the day together."

And do what?, I thought. When I got back, it took her seven weeks to start sleeping with me, That came on a strictly special occasion basis, and just one carefully negotiated occasion had risen to that level of specialness so far. Then she got up. Without looking back, she padded back down to the couch to sleep among her familiars.

Melanie loved her ancient cat, a smelly, mat-furred, orange tabby she had cared for since he got squashed in the road as a kitten, and miraculously survived. Still furious about losing his balls to domestic requirements, he hobbled sway-bellied around the house, spraying his resentment liberally. When he stomped onto my lap and hosed hot piss all over my chest—a thing that had happened more times than physical romance since my deployment ended—Mel was always very solicitous about the rage and confusion of the kitty.

"He's old, he doesn't understand," she would say, cooing at Tigger and stroking his head.

She liked falling asleep on the couch with the cat for a comforter and the TV muttering goodnight.

"I guess I just got used to it this way," she said. "You were gone for a year."

Ten months and I had gotten used to sleeping in tin cans with men, but I for one was more than ready to make the switch. On her more honest occasions, Melanie considered the relaxing ambiguity of intercontinental mash notes, and admitted that she may have liked the concept of me returning better than my physical remanifestation at the house she had named "Cat Mountain."

There was a sign on the door proclaiming that ranch-style name. I had carved it for her with a router and chisels a few years earlier out of old growth, straight-grain fir, brushing on four coats of spar varnish.

Not that sleeping arrangements made much difference, one way or the other. My doctor had prescribed a small bottle of pills—with a large co-pay required—that were specially formulated to ram the lead back into my pencil. Levitra, or something generically akin. It's more legitimate to buy it from a pharmacy than the back of a men's magazine, as far as I know.

After chomping through half the bottle, I pretty much gave up on that. Melanie didn't seem at all disappointed, and I tried not to notice that.

So very funny, in a not-ha-ha kind of way: after spending my whole adult life sniffing after women, wondering what I was missing like every other monogamous male, I found myself perched at the latter edge of my prime, looking fairly rugged and catching not a few flirty looks and not giving a fart in a high wind about it. Not giving a fart in a high wind about much of anything, really. Honor and glory and courage and pussy-hunting: all recycled high school football crap. Funny, funny world—bitter, ugly and malevolent, but funny indeed.

There was also the mystery of that drugstore box, labeled "EPT," that I found under her side of the double-sink vanity. It was still in the shrink wrap, so I couldn't tell if it was old, but its expiration date hadn't rolled around yet. I wondered when she had bought that.

And yeah, I wondered why.

Here we were, then, spending the day together.

"Well, if I fall off the roof, someone needs to be here," I told her.

I didn't cop to my difficulty just getting out the door when she wasn't home, or that my spite for the quiet, empty, shit-reeking house was exceeded only by my wish to avoid the skull-rattling inanity of daytime TV. I heard too much of myself to function when I was home alone, and I could hear other things, too. People screamed in the back of my head, sometimes, and maybe they always would. I would get off track, lose my way, and sit transfixed in front of the computer, wondering why I was there, until my eyes hurt so much I would flee downstairs and look longingly at the front door.

Anyway, if the roof was going to get done, it had to be when she was here.

Right out in the open.

For ten years, that roof got cleaned twice each year: once in autumn, once in spring. Then, when I decided to give it one more go in the Reserves, I dropped out of the Pacific Northwest and trained my way across the backwater southern states of West Virginia, North Carolina, Arkansas and Georgia, and straight on into one of our ongoing series of undeclared wars.

Now it was autumn—I refused to even think the word "fall"—and for the first time since the house was new I hadn't cleaned the roof in over a year. I slow-footed it up our massive, overweight stepladder. A boondoggle, I thought when she bought it for me new, but it was much steadier than the dinged-up 24-foot extension ladder I kyped from the wreckage of our old company. Carefully, I eased over the eaves and onto the rooftop of the garage. Not too bad so far.

Getting up slowly, keeping my knees bent—hurt more than they used to, and made more noise, but that's life and priests and other thanatophiles insist it beats the alternative—I hiked to the peak of the garage roof. I turned my broadening butt toward the main house roof, gave a hop and heaved myself up to a sitting position on the next level up. That was the plan I had visualized, anyway, but it's a rare plan that survives the collision with reality. When I pulled my knees up after the hop, something got in the way.

It was the belly. I hadn't gotten used to it yet. Even though I watched it wobbling, buttery white under the dark winter fur, over the vanity sink every morning when I looked in the mirror to shave, it was still a stranger and not properly integrated into my flow. We were not acclimatized to each other, me and the belly. I was persistently aware of the flat sheath of military muscle underneath, atrophying slowly away but still flickering at the edge of my awareness like a phantom limb.

Now the belly was frankly annoying, getting in the way, and obstructing my mission. The belly was pissing me off.

"Gym tomorrow," I promised the recently-less-integrated componentry of my musculoskeletal system, "without fail."

But right now, a little belly discipline was called for. Sucking in the gut, I bent my legs to a half squat, kept my hands on the roof edge behind me, hopped with everything I had and *snapped* my knees up to my chest, squashing in enough quilted gut to drive the breath out of my lungs but gaining a precarious sphincter-hold just uphill of the gutter. A little huckle of the arms and legs and butt and I could sprawl there, looking up, and pant for a moment. Cardio capacity shot to hell, but okay so far. A tidbit of dry leaf blew across the roof and caught in my stubble, where I ignored it.

I'd always enjoyed the roof work. For one thing, our house was a "view home" of Lake Washington, as promised by our preening real estate agent, only when I straddled the peak of our roof and peered at the green-gray water slice to the right of our neighbor's massive cedar. When we were new to the house and still learning the neighborhood, I liked to scramble around up there, standing tanned and shirtless and making a little extra noise when someone walked by so they could see a true householder fighting the good fight against decay and rot.

It felt like marching through villages in the cold war Republic of Korea when I was just a kid like Will, or patrolling rubble-ized Iraqi cities as a recycled aulde pharte searching for weapon smugglers along the Syrian border: happy to put my hand in and make a difference, proud to be seen doing it.

Had to maintain that upper perimeter against rain.

In Lake Forest Park, moss never sleeps. The creeping vegetable insurgency hadn't wasted any time on the back slope of our roof. Cresting the rise, I looked down over a verdant fungal field, fluffy emerald billows bridging shingles in a contiguous furry swath.

Right, then. Out with the stainless steel brush, time to bust moss. I was in silhouette up there, but you can't be cautious about everything, all the time. Life is what happens on the roof, in the ring, outside the wire. The numbness stops when it's saturated with Technicolor fear. Fear happens where there's focus. And a man lives to focus, lives through his focused, attentive, busy working hands.

The army announces that it's "assuming some risk" when it commits living troops to something absurdly dangerous in order to score a tactical point—or, sometimes, just a psychological one. An enemy who smells a commander's lack of resolve will assume he's closing in on victory, and redouble his efforts. At least, that's how we'd always played it.

So what looked like tactically sound, safe-margin strategies of overwhelming force were discarded along with the old-school generals—including a secretary of state—who had advocated them. You go to war with the army you have, or anyway a jumpy little slice of it, so we rarely mobilized overwhelming force. There was too much ground to cover, too many people to talk to and mayors to advise and police chiefs to discipline and *sheikhs* to buy off, too big an agenda for too few soldiers.

So instead, we went crazy places and did crazy things to jack up Ali Baba: "Shit, man—you'll *never* be crazier 'n' us." I was never a big picture strategist or a general. I can't tell you what the thinking was, only what we did.

How do you out-crazy people who finance suicide bombing of funerals and weddings, and stitch corpses full of flake TNT to leave by the fountain in the public square? By taunting them with amplified insults to their manhood, by putting yourself out there, by running slow and ignoring fire because they were such crappy shots. You hunted Ali through his own neighborhood, invited yourselves into his house, bundled his women into a side room and jacked him up half naked in his own dirty stone courtyard to snap digital pictures over his sorry-ass, rusted Chinese AK and Czech 9mm pistol.

Or sometimes more. In tracks and trucks and Kevlar hats, we came storming out of the nation that invented drive-by shootings and arena football, a country that thinks rugby is a pansy game and soccer is for girls, and we weren't about to be out-crazed by a motley bunch of amateurs in stained man-dresses and gay-ass head rags.

You did what you had to do, and you kept up the pressure, and you didn't stop to think about it even for a moment because that. Was. Not. The. Time.

I sometimes wondered when the time would come.

This wasn't it, obviously. This was the day I assumed some risk of my own, up there on the roof where I had many times resolved and many times failed to bolt down a tie-off for a fall arrest.

This was the day I thanked God for my busy hands.

My forepaws, unlike the belly, weren't complete strangers to me. They were just as rawboned and red-knuckled as when I left, strong-thumbed with short fingers and calluses edging my thick palms at the base of each finger. Boxer's fractures and embedded glass chips and one wayward chisel slip that nicked an artery, spraying the walls and floor and water heater in our garage.

Same old aches, plus a few new ones, sounding off in a digital roll call. For awhile there, I wasn't entirely sure they'd be with me my whole life, but events and my hands were looking better now as I prowled the rooftop, predator of moss.

When my slip-on Pay-Less shoe slithered out from under me on the snotty greenery, it looked like I had found out when my time would come. My foot vanished out from under me and the shoe flipped completely off, looping down into the backyard. My left hip pounded into the roof with a boom that made my IED-pulped eardrum shrill into my head like a security alarm. Sliding down the gritty shingles toward the backside gutter, I left a gooey little trail of smeared blood and skin. Over the edge was a 38-foot drop-off to our fall-away backyard and the dark, mapled Elks Club woodlot sloping down beyond the fence.

Like a combat zone abroad and not one bit like a TV war serial, there was no screaming. I clawed for a hold and fought for my life in a workmanlike way. A pure focus of pre-cognitive reaction was required and as many times before, it came to me automatically.

In the kitchen, I heard Melanie singing and thought of her iconic smile as I had thought of it so many times. Occasionally, I thought it would be my last remote view of her, my sacred statuette, posed in the best-lit and most-visited crèche of my mind. One leg waved, roach-like, over the sucker-tree void. My right knee was jammed into the sagging gutter the way we'd dig our fingers into a detainee's shoulder to steer them, blindfolded and staggering in their *dish-dashas* and rubber sandals, to a Stryker armored vehicle for safe passage away from the snap and whistle of international disagreement and back to the FOB for processing. I wouldn't miss them, or their country, or the horse I rode in on.

I held on, and then the other shoe dropped, thumping quietly into the wet fall leaves below. When the dark wave of futility washed over me, I let go.

Just let it all go.

Fear overrode my system with a jerk like sudden voltage. The Fear rode a pale horse, and carried death in its bony claw. Hell followed after just as it was written, and Hell was the neighborhood of everyone I knew: charred stumps and meaty exit wounds and child damagers, business cheaters and sour bureaucrats, bad sergeants and murderous insurgents and politicized officers and spooks with retirement accounts; the grim and the bitter, the cheerful and the stupid, the too-young just-married virtual virgins; the fat, the old, the egotistical, the simply inadequate.

They smiled at me and beckoned; they called out my name. Enemies and allies, obstacles and assistants, the good and the bad and the lost and the doomed. They had always been my family, after all, and my family reached up for me then. They welcomed me down with their open, rotting arms.

It came to me that I was the boon companion of the damned—self-condemned like the rest of those losers, all the sad cases who got a "No Go" on navigation because they couldn't operate a simple moral compass and I cried, there at the edge.

Skidding, I bawled like a goat, sobbing for them and for myself, bleeding saltwater from my eyes into the fecund, spongiform muck of a slowly failing gutter, quavering with the fear I never allowed on-mission, never showed to my guys when they were shaking after a firefight because they would still have to go where I ordered them to go, next time and every time.

They would have to go the way Will went, and Will did. And Will rode back on a litter, surrounded by beds full of broken people and boxes full of people parts that all the king's Strykers and all the king's men never could put back together again.

Now maybe I could go, too. Maybe I could lay down that ruck and join my brothers, while my wife cooked rich, beef noodle winter soup and sang in the kitchen and I enjoyed one last slot view of Lake Washington, just past my neighbor's cedar.

Slip-sliding away, my groping hand brushed against a thing. Workmanlike and strong, the hand focused its mindless competence reflexively, and I looked and saw that I had clenched the rubber tube of a roof vent in my relentless grip.

The vent was not strong. Mossy shingles to either side bulged from the load.

No pressure.

I moved slowly, very slowly, as perfectly undistracted and Zen-like as a bullfrog tracking flies. Flattening and spreading along the creaking gutter, my belly distributed load widely enough to avert a single point of failure. Inching my way back up, knees crackling with crepitus and faded muscles shaking at maximum output, I started to believe I might complete this mission after all.

Once back up on the rooftop, I rolled onto my back and fell automatically into an ecstatic, post-mission blur. Ice-cold adrenaline ebbed away as I padded carefully back across the crown, back to the ladder top in my filthy socks.

It felt like riding back to FOB Sykes, standing tall in the air guard hatch of a clanging, booming Stryker with a hot wind in my face, happy to crack a few more bad jokes over the intercom with my immortal fellows after once again anointing each other copiously with bulletproof unguent in the midst of the endless, redundant sacrifices practiced every day in humanity's thousand temples of death.

My name would not adorn the litany. Not this day, and there is nothing like that high.

Grooving on senses still raised to battle pitch, I heard crickets walking over my tinnitus; my cloudy eyes narrowed with the clear focus of a hunting hawk. From the top of my Little

Giant, I read from Alana's yard signs across the street: "Support our troops! Bring 'em home NOW!," and, "No Blood for Oil!"

Well, no blood for moss today, anyway.

When my feet touched down on solid driveway asphalt, I pulled off my dish gloves with a wet snap and wiped my face, surprised to find my whiskers soaking wet.

Had I actually cried, after all that time? Sergeants don't cry. Wondering who had time for that, I struck my ladder and hauled it into the garage. Not slinking like a victim; moving like a man. Walking in daylight, not skulking in alleyways; not prowling the green-tinged night in the armor and cat's eyes of a comic book hero, some low-rent Batman without the cave, the millions or the *savoir faire*. A vampire no more.

It was sinking in that those dead kids' boots and rifles wouldn't leave my mind anytime soon, not unless I tucked my compact Glock 19 under my stubbly chin and blew them straight out of there along with everything else. Neither would the kid with a rifle that I shot in the shadows ("There's your *moussasa*, you little fucker!"), or a lot of others. They were all going to live with me for a long time. Probably forever. I would have to force my mind and heart to grow and accommodate them, and it would hurt worse than any Osgood Slaughter's Disease.

There is no exorcism of the past. You have no choice but to accept what has already happened. Thinking maybe I shouldn't need dead guys to point that out for me, I shucked off my shoes and strode into our four-bedroom, 2.5-bath, nearly empty house that smelt of meat and noodles.

"Hey, sweetie," I said. "I'm 'onna hafta finish up later."

"Oh, good. Dinner will be ready in half an hour.

"Are you okay? Why is your face so red? Take your dirty pants off before you sit on the couch. Not yet—you need to take out the recycling. Can I fix you a quick snack while dinner's cooking? I don't suppose you put the suets up for the birds—"

"Yeah," I interrupted her. "I'm fine."

I stopped to consider my sleek, fierce Melanie. Freed from the cramped little niche of my mind, her face was vibrant, moon-shaped and generous. Her body, warm and present beyond conceptual nostalgia, brimmed warm with our shared life. Her prattling domestic routines weren't background static but the davit I tied off to, to keep from floating away.

I put my hands on her lean hips. A man's working hands.

"I'm actually fine."

Her scraggly orange cat rubbed on my ankles, then bit me playfully through my sock. Mel put her hands up, gently cupping my raspy cheeks.

"Do you want a beer before dinner? I think you deserve one."

"No, thank you, sweetie." I looked at her and wanted to kiss her, but I couldn't stop looking just yet. Maybe we'd have some time left for kissing, after all. Maybe time for other things. A moment of time to hold life in our hands while we could. I had a pretty wife, capable hands, and a loaded pistol sitting on my handmade nightstand.

"I'm really just fine."

NOTHING BETTER TO DO

*...not only are they commemorated by columns and
inscriptions, but there dwells also an unwritten memorial of
them, graven not on stone but in the hearts of men.*

—Thucydides, *The Funeral Oration of Pericles*

We were most of the way there when a radio announcer
told his audience, "Hey, it's Memorial Day Weekend—you don't
have anything better to do."

Then he threw on some more oldies, and some of them
were goodies, and we drove east across the Maple Valley through
the cool gray rain, humming a little to his program.

> *Ain't no mountain high enough*
> *Ain't no valley low enough*
> *Ain't no river wide enough*
> *To keep me away from you, babe*

I smiled over at Melanie, who had quit humming and
commenced belting out the chorus. Her voice sounded brittle
but pretty across the heated cab.

"Last May, I was itching to get out of Iraq," I reminded her. "Right now, I'm pretty happy to not have anything better to do.

"What do those directions say from here?"

Melanie sang in a clear, sweet voice when she was contented, but she interrupted herself then.

"We need to find James Street in Kent, then go up the hill and keep going several miles further.

"It's just past Tahoma High School."

We climbed the hill out of Kent. Pretty soon, the mini-malls and service stations of western Washington suburbia gave way to a winding road through rolling hills dotted with pastures, clots of thicket and elaborate, horse-acre ranchettes. It was beautiful countryside for those as could afford it. A few poorly maintained older farms hung on, hoping to outwait the market.

We began to see signs encouraging us on to the site "WHERE HEROES REST."

Half a mile past Tahoma High School, with its colorful steel roof slanted in the pole barn styling that used to be admired as "Northwest Modern" before we tumbled to the reality of its cost-effective imperative, a broad, asphalted entrance welcomed drivers into Tahoma National Cemetery.

There are rules posted there, bolted to burly steel signposts adjacent to every agglomeration of grave markers, but they hardly seemed necessary on the Sunday before Memorial Day. Among families patrolling the grounds in reverent clusters, a group of 35 high schoolers industriously scrubbed the headstones of men and women unknown to them.

Rumors of graveside social protests had reached the Northwest, spurring the founding of Oregon and Washington chapters of the Patriot Guard ("Riding With Respect"), but such crimes against families' grief seem to be of other places and other people. At Tahoma, a civil and political ceasefire naturally prevailed as it naturally should.

Mel and I searched the stones, finding a number of recent interments. Jewish chaplains from World War II, bakers from Vietnam, aircrews blown out of the sky by mechanical malfunction, and those who served survived to serve as citizens and die as veterans. Not the stone I was looking for.

Gently but persistently, the rain drew grass from the bones of soldiers. I walked through it for some time, dressed in my late father-in-law's dense wool cardigan and a drab hat with my oxidized Combat Action Badge pinned to the crown. Melanie and I spoke softly over some of our discoveries, tiny insights into past lives through the solid granite windows laid out on the plush lawn.

My shoes leaked. Her father's sweater outgassed lanolin fumes. Falling water ran from the brim of my hat as I mumbled along, chasing ghosts. Finally, Melanie reached out from under her umbrella to pull at my sleeve.

"Jack, I don't want you getting in the car if you're all wet."

"Don't worry about it," I mumbled absently. "I'll take off the sweater before I get in."

My agenda beyond this simple Sunday visit was unshared.

Locally-linked combat deaths from our Global War On Terror had begun to stack up early. Somewhere on this ground, an operator from the 1st Special Forces Group at Fort Lewis lay buried. A commo sergeant, he was the first U.S. soldier to be killed in Afghanistan under the rubric of Operation Enduring Freedom.

There was also, I knew, an army non-commissioned officer from the Olympic Peninsula navy town of Bremerton, but I couldn't find him, either.

Across the wide boulevard, I saw a man in a navy blue work jacket and billed cap, exiting a small utility vehicle that had headstones stacked carefully in its bed beneath its spindly davit hoist. I headed toward him.

"Jack…?"

"I'll be right back," I assured her. My wife was becoming impatient with my unexplained errand, and I was becoming impatient with my wife, and I needed information.

"Excuse me, sir?"

He immediately stopped his errand, watching me with salt and pepper patience.

"Can I help?"

Because I had a catch in my throat that I couldn't quite clear, I just stammered and croaked at him the best I could while he listened.

"I-I'm not sure. I need to find a recent… it was October. In 2004. October 2004. A staff sergeant… was killed in Mosul…?"

"Do you have his name?" He unfurled a thick sheaf of information typed in lists. African-American, he was about my height, twenty years older and more fit, wearing a navy blue maintenance jacket and a gray mustache under his blue baseball cap.

"He was... I can't... I was there.

"I can't remember, but I was there. A staff sergeant. An IED." I looked at the ground, frustrated with myself. My tattered memory embarrassed me. I could still bench press anvils, but I couldn't find my way through a shopping mall or keep track of basic bills. Wearing the body of a retired baseball jock made my mental fits and starts feel like driving a custom-painted Camaro with a Johnny popper under the hood.

"I'm sorry."

"Hey," he said. "That must have been a hard day."

When I raised my head, he was looking at me with kindness and pointing back beyond the toiling high schoolers. A Vietnam service medal was embroidered onto the crown of his ball cap.

"At the end of that area, where the first row starts out with just a couple stones—see there? That row and the next four rows coming this way are all recent combat funerals.

"You could look there. Sure you don't remember the exact date?"

He flipped pages until he got to October of '04. There were so many names on the sheets. He must have held a quarter-ream of paper in his hands.

"I don't remember much of anything these days, but I'll know it when I see it."

I reached out my hand, and he took off his blue rubber-tipped Atlas work glove and shook it.

"Thank you, sir."

"God bless you," he answered, "and good luck."

I range-walked toward the far end of the stone garden where he had pointed. Melanie hurried to catch up, slipped on the wet grass and almost put my eye out with her umbrella.

"This is the wrong way, I think," she said urgently. "The dates aren't going the right way. These are older stones."

"Just give me a minute, please."

The second stone in the fourth row had yellow flowers all around it. His family had been there, industriously obscuring his name with the petals of their sorrow and affection, but I knew the date when I saw it: October 11.

That was the date of my team's first significant firefight. Our first SVBIED. Russ's first kill. The day my surviving daughter turned 14. The day SSG Michael L. Burbank, a brave man who left his family in Bremerton to fight in his country's name in a raddled, Allah-forsaken, oil-cursed dustbowl, was killed by a whizzing chunk of hot shrapnel that arrowed from an exploding truck straight through his throat and into his *medulla oblongata* while he stood vigilant watch in the hatch of a Stryker armored vehicle.

SSG Burbank was by all accounts a fine soldier, aggressive and wily and tough. He took action when necessary, and led from the front. He also took reasonable precautions, but there's no ducking that.

The day he died was the day of Operation Block Party II. It was scheduled to be 1-14 Cavalry's last major operation; they were due to ship home in less than two weeks with the rest of 3-2 Stryker Brigade Combat Team.

My team, like the rest of our detachment, could wear a combat patch from either the 2nd Infantry "First to Fight" Division or the 25th Infantry "Tropic Lightning" Division. In memory of SSG Burbank, each member of our team put on the Second ID Indianhead patch. The 1-25 cav officers we served with never forgave us for it, but 3-2 SBCT[36] was the first unit with which we saw combat.

Russ had an aluminum bracelet engraved with Michael Burbank's name, and he never took it off.

I stood for a few moments in front of the Burbank grave marker. Like thousands of other military markers around the country, it is no hubris-fueled monument to ego. But it is not humble, either—not humble in the sense of one who lays down without a fight, or lurks and lags until others take charge. It is not fancy. It is not preening.

It is proud.

I reached into my sweater pocket and found the gleaming, dress-finish Combat Action Badge that Doog had slipped me the day of our award ceremony at an American Legion Hall smelling of stale cigarettes and pine oil. I had never opened it, never pinned it to my dress green blouse. Shucking off its plastic wrap, I pulled it off the white cardboard, re-set its

---

[36] Stryker Brigade Combat Team, then a new formation in the army's ongoing process of "transformation," organized around the Stryker eight-wheel-drive armored vehicle. Stykers were affectionately nicknamed "Kevlar coffins."

turtles on the back pins, and placed it carefully on top of his headstone.

Then I took two steps back and saluted a man who gave more than I ever had to, indeed gave more than any citizen reading these words. That little courtesy, that formal acknowledgement, was all I had to give back to Michael Burbank.

We saluted a lot of boots, spurs, Stetsons, helmets and rifles before we left that country. Fighting in wars turned out to be just about as dangerous as it sounds. But because of the confusion of one supported unit being replaced by another, we missed the field memorial service for SSG Burbank. It would have been our first.

Why did I give my CAB to him? Seems presumptuous, I suppose—he wasn't kin to me. We weren't in the same unit. Never even met, in fact.

Michael Burbank earned that Combat Action Badge well before we watched him earn his Purple Heart, but he died before the CAB was ever approved for issue. It never graced his uniform and wouldn't have been awarded posthumously alongside his Purple Heart and medal for valor. It wasn't invented and approved for wear until months after his death.

Still, I left that small, never-meaningless token for him and allowed myself to hope that his family would find it before cemetery staff removed it, so that they might know that somewhere a stranger remembered their son with gratitude, and with respect.

My glasses were fogging, probably from the rain. Mel came over to me, sniffling. She had found the markers of two soldiers recently KIA, one 20 and the other 21 years old.

"They were so young," she said. "So young."

She sobbed quietly.

"They never had their chance to make their mark in this world."

I started walking back to the car, unaccountably annoyed. She pulled alongside, hustling to keep up.

"They didn't have the chance—"

"I heard you," I growled, bitter and cranky and trying to keep the quaver out of my voice.

"Like Hell they didn't.

"Who do you know who made a bigger mark? Your B-school buddies? Your lawyer friends? *Ken-freakin'-Lay?*

"A soldier's mark will last forever."

It won't, of course.

Empires fall, and so do constitutional republics. We're a blip on the vast span of human time, which itself is barely a bug stain on the windshield of geologic time, itself only a one-act play on the cosmic stage. *Look on me, ye mighty, and despair,* screamed Ozymandias, lying tumbled and alone in the desert wind. None of us is all that special. None of us carries more of the universe in us than the next guy.

Neither SSG Burbank, nor the kids resting near him, nor the equally young kids on my team or any of the other hundreds of thousands of service members who bet it all on Uncle Sam's craps table did it for fame and glory, anyway. You can't be too far along a military arc before you figure out that this is no game for divas and prima donnas.

No good deed goes unpunished, and life in the army is fair once a day at quarter past never. Soldiers learn to do the right thing not to get a cookie, or even to stay out of trouble. They remind each other to remind each other to act right, to pay attention to detail, to watch out for their buddy, not to be whack. They pick up their weapons and run to the sound of the guns, bitching every step of the way. They do the right thing because it's the right thing, even when it's hard.

Especially when it's hard.

Where do we find such men? Such women? Such warriors?

Unlike the millionaire next door, the soldier next door is uncelebrated by commerce and culture. He is the sheepdog, the ranger, the sentry who walks our walls. She is the corpsman, the driver, the mate who patrols our harbors. It was my brief privilege to stand with—not the prettiest people, nor the best educated or most flossily advantaged—but the very best people my country could offer up.

One day, perhaps I will be honored to lie beside them.

In the meantime, allow me to persist in this unpleasant reminder: the supply of such courage in the land of the free, home of the brave currently represents less than one percent of our God-graced population.

"It's like that warrior hall," Mel said quietly, just before we drove out of the green hills to infiltrate the gritty valley sprawl of Unocals, VFW halls and Westernco doughnut shops that made up the central area of Kent.

"Where the Viking warriors went."

"Walhalla?," I asked her.

"Yes. The Valhalla."

She was reaching a little, trying to connect with my Swedish forebears. I nodded, but Walhalla wasn't what I thought of in the context of those emerald acres quietly overlooking Mt. Rainier.

With its tottering, silvered widows bearing fragrant floral displays and its quiet, granitic reminders standing watch in regular rows, Tahoma sounded a more pacific echo of war than that festive berserker hall of Nordic myth.

We remember our heroes differently now, and classify heroism in nuanced ways. At Tahoma, epitaphs including "Beloved Grandfather," "Scholar" and "Music Man" stand in proud formation alongside the stones marking those who fell in battle. Men and women who returned from war to forge ploughshares and build are honored in the same manner, with the same martial discipline and careful dignity afforded to their kin, as those who followed Mars pounding and careening down that short, bright-burning detour. A Civil War lieutenant of colored troops, posthumously honored with the Congressional Medal of Honor, and a PFC who returned from the "forgotten war" in Korea to live out the full span of his years lie in egalitarian serenity in this still and peaceful place.

I know a man or two in Walhalla, to be sure. It isn't hard to smile, imagining them cheerfully battling each day only to be healed at eventide, hoisting a toast to triumph and tearing bites from roasted game served by laughing wenches who make 72 veiled virgins look like a fistful of dried raisins, but that isn't the metaphor for Tahoma.

If any archaic model applies, it is the Elysian fields, wide and vibrant, as open to Plato and to Homer as to Perseus and Agamemnon. The mortal remains of combat-killed generals and foot soldiers lie here interspersed with those of sailors who returned from war to found businesses and raise children, and to kibitz on the raising of their children's children. There is true democracy here, as pure an example as has existed since the antique coining of the word.

And there is peace.

One can only pray that our heroes walk a field much like this one, vital and alive with birdsong and respectful endeavor, temperate and placid with measured prudence.

Not a battlefield, not a parade ground or a training field. A field where no mortars fall, where the streets never explode and no slugs whine past, and where no soldier ever works his back out, filling sandbags in the sun.

STOPLIGHT EPILOGUE

Oh, come on! People are fungible.

—Donald Rumsfeld, U.S. Secretary of Defense

We were almost home when a round number fell out of the radio.

I put my hand up to my mouth, remembered that I don't smoke anymore, and put it back on the steering wheel. The traffic light ahead flashed to red, and we all stopped together.

Looking straight ahead, I mumbled, "By the time I got to Camp Freedom, KBR had two kills."

A year or lifetime before, I had walked into one of the army's recently de-Saddamed palaces with my freshly laminated Task Force Olympia access badge, a sort of all-areas backstage pass to war, and flipped through the safety bulletin pinned up on the polished, gray-veined marble of the lobby wall. Three pages down, the notice caught my eye.

"What? Who?" Maybe she hadn't been listening to the radio show, or maybe she was still listening. Solemn voices continued out of our dashboard, confirming the toll.

"Kellogg, Brown and Root," I said. "They had two kills."

We were newbies then, with big eyes in our swiveling heads. Hot chicks from the CIA carried Glocks to lunch, where mortars fell into the mess tent from over the Tigris River. You could buy desiccated Havana cigars and fresh *chai* in the castle's basement lobby; trade American Camels to South African mercenaries from the next pad over for whiskey and beer. Rogue Kurds busily translated English into Arabic for us to broadcast through dusty American loudspeakers in order to influence Sunni insurgents roaming the Shiite neighborhoods, who bombed us anyway so we shot at them in the international language.

Nothing was believable. Just as it seemed incredible to her, being so removed from her world.

"KBR lost two people?" Melanie's forehead wrinkled up. She was from Houston. A highway on the outskirts of Houston has a whole bypass dedicated to the KBR employee parking lot. "How?," she asked.

"*Killed* two people," I corrected her.

I hated traffic jams. I looked every which way, drumming my thumbs on the steering wheel, pounding rim shots the way my mom used to do after her divorce.

I had forgotten all about those two. Most taxpayers probably had. I wondered what my army had told their families.

"Iraqis?" She worried about such things.

"GIs." I wondered whether they were counted in this day's Big Number.

"KBR killed two *soldiers?*

"How?"

The radio informed us that the Senate had observed 22 somber seconds of silence. Each Senator who was on the floor that day devoted a full eleven-thousandths of one second—on the clock—to each soldier killed in Iraq. They are a deliberative body.

"Two guys were electrocuted in the showers," I said. "Two different FOBs in Mosul."

"To *death?*," she asked.

"Yeah. That's what 'electrocuted' means."

I wondered if those two names would ever be read out in the Senate. I wondered if someday all 2,000 of them would be read out to that august body. Back then, 2,000 seemed like a very large number. Probably even to the Senate, which had many pressing issues to consider.

It would take a long time, and maybe there was no point in looking back. Time is precious, never to be squandered. Liberals wanted to Move On, while conservatives insisted we "get over it." If we could all just agree that there was no time to waste, we could keep moving forward together. Even our army had a slogan for it: "Drive on!"

"Oh, my God, that's terrible!," Melanie said. "We never heard about that on the news."

Taking another pull on my imaginary cigarette, I said, "Yeah.

"How 'bout that?"

The light turned green.

We drove on.

PHOENIX

The White Man will never be alone. Let him be just and deal kindly with my people, for the dead are not powerless—dead, I say?

There is no death. Only a change of worlds.

—Chief Sealth (*Duwamish tribe, possibly apocryphal*)

American Lake Veterans Administration Hospital is a peaceful refuge dotted with tall Douglas firs and Western hemlock, pale Mission-style buildings, rusty Quonset huts leftover and condemned, and rotting polychrome totem poles. ALVAH brings together on one campus the ambience of a hospital, nursing home and mental ward, with the cutting-edge style of a 1973 bowling league.

It's a sanctuary where the only shrieks drift upshore from American Lake and signify nothing more than sunburnt teens in a fiberglass hull, arcing back to pick up a fallen water skier. They take care of their own. They leave no skier behind.

You can watch the water sports from the bank, but your feet will stay dry by decree. The hospital staff lined its lake frontage with dog fence years ago after a mental health patient drowned himself in the hospital's backyard. The only gate in the fence leads to a small, well-tended dock. A sign on the gate, white-lettered over brown wood in the style of our national parks, reads, "THIS FISHING DOCK IS FOR AUTHORIZED AND SUPERVISED PATIENTS ONLY." The comprehensive list of rules following this proclamation seems redundant for patients who are authorized and supervised; detected, selected and rejected.

In a 16-foot aluminum boat with amidships steering station, a dark-haired man trolled up and down the summer waters, backward and forward in front of the fishing dock. I raised my hand to him, and he stared at me for a moment. Then he turned his boat away from the bank. He seemed appointed to embody the well-begged question: was the fence protecting us, or the people in their boats?

Because it is a caretaking institution, ALVAH naturally attracts those who need someone to take care of them. That's its mission, what it is intended for, why it was constructed in the first place at no doubt exorbitant taxpayer expense.

And they are here, those people. If you build it, they will come, shuffling downcast and stooped from building to building, searching for a wisp of remembered life among the cages of a zombie zoo that, should fashionable teens ever volunteer here for a day or two, would cause even the most withdrawn of Goths to rethink their shimmering, exquisitely tuned teen angst. If, that is, they had time to volunteer between parties energized by competitive ennui.

Patients who sift down the social strata to land here following round after round of soul-stunting, hyper-formalized institutional begging, often come to resemble a particular archetype: regardless of ethnicity, they are moist and pale as maggots, plump and soft and helpless as silkworm grubs.

If I arrived early for a morning appointment, I might repair to the canteen for a "Sausage Max" and a large, black coffee: a pint of acidic Folgers in a flexible foam cup for a buck. No one there could afford—financially or philosophically—to be as hip as Starbuckin' Seattleites. They spooked around the grounds, wearing random surplus knickknacks and thin shirts from the campus convenience store and embroidered ball caps marked with the names of ships and specialties, medals and service branches. They sat out on the benches in Bermuda shorts and camouflage ponchos over Gore-Tex-lined Bellevue winter boots, next to stinking red butt cans, smoking hard in the gentle rain.

In the canteen, I heard a quavering skeleton composed of little more than shell fragments and paddy water noisily announce to the assembled fried food seekers that "They" had almost stopped his methadone because he messed up his own paperwork, but he soon calmed down and lapsed back into his wheelchair to stare at the prominent bones of his knees.

They were too old, these vets, too young, too thin or fat to be my peer group. Too fucked up, really. They were not me, and I was not them.

Not needy, not stumbling, not broken: not me!

On my fourth visit, after my coffee and before I went up to the outpatient floor of the mental health center again to hear Björn tell me again that I wasn't going to start improving until I admitted that I needed to start healing, I visited the latrine adjacent to the canteen. Holding the door for a moment to let an African American gentleman pass out, I did my business and washed up in front of the mirror.

The guy looking back at me wore a cheap, black, Chinese-stitched baseball cap, silkscreened with an image of the USACAPOC[37] patch. Over a quarter-inch of stubble running down his rusty neck into an army-issue zipper fleece that was too hot for this day, the man in the mirror looked back at me with hollow, glittery eyes. I pitied him a little, but wouldn't have wanted to see him stumbling down a sidewalk in my neighborhood to trip over the obvious conclusion.

I am that guy. I am these men and these women, and they are me: white trash huddled with our black brothers, trying to dream ourselves safe in our fortified time capsule.

On my counselor's advice, I went to mess around at the Seattle VA for a couple of days. They have a "Deployment Clinic" there, whatever the fuck that means. Seems like it should be called a "Redeployment Clinic" since you go there after you get back. Or some of us do, anyway.

---

[37] U.S. Army Civil Affairs and Psychological Operations Command

The first day, I talked to a doctor, who filled out some forms. The second day, I filled out 32 pages of forms, donated four vials of blood to science, and shat in a clear plastic beaker for the nice Filipina at the lab window.

First day's notes:

Went down to the Seattle VA hospital today, because my counselor at the American Lake nut hatch sort of insisted that I go and add my statistics to their Deployment Clinic. Duty to other vets, etc. Duty is never done; it just evolves through time.

There are a lot of wheelchairs and crutches and prostheses to walk by when you report to the VA. Standing in the lobby waiting for my turn at the info desk, I felt kind of funny about it.

It's not like I got shot up or anything. I'm whole and can ride down there on a motorcycle.

Street cred for hopped-up Subarus comes from a turbocharger and nitrous oxide injection; for soldiers, it's a Combat Infantry Badge. But at the VA hospital, credibility comes bundled inside a gurgling colostomy bag.

Hearing a familiar voice and noting the severe duck feet of the guy in front of me, I smacked him hard on the shoulder and said, "HEY, you ugly bastard!"

The guy was big and built, and when he spun around and hugged me, I thought he'd spring a rib. Crutching his way into the lobby, a dark gray Vietnam vet smiled knowingly at us.

Big Danny was on a slightly different drug regimen than I was, but we were both trying to get the VA to spring for our prescriptions (no joy so far, for either of us). Mine was Welbutrin. It smelled vaguely like yogurt and was as often used for D&A addictions as for depression.

Maybe they were going for a two-fer.

I can't remember what Danny's was—Depakote, maybe?—but then I can't remember much of anything these days. If I missed a dose of W, the skin on my forearms burned and I got twitchy and paranoid, so I learned to keep little stashes of it in various places so as not to be caught short by my treacherous, shredded memory.

Both our wives insisted that we not miss a dose, because that was when some of the bad things happened. Sometimes, of course, they happened anyway. Melanie got tired of holes caved into drywall, smashed hollow core doors, knuckle marks in our steel-clad front door and boxer's fractures that took weeks to heal. She couldn't believe what she was seeing the night I tried to shut her up by smashing all the letters out of my computer keyboard with my forehead.

So the meds were a good thing, really. Several times, they damped down my reflexive red-hot fury when Melanie abruptly turned up the radio and said, "Let's just not talk for awhile."

"Do you have any idea how much it pisses me off when you do that?," I'd ask her.

"Everything pisses you off these days."

I'd heard that before. It pissed me off every time.

It was a sunny afternoon in Mosul, where they have a lot of those, when Big Danny earned the nickname that stuck to him throughout his tour.

Danny was patrolling with the infantry, a one-man PSYOP team as usual, when his platoon identified a small knot of terrorists and engaged them. Two men were neutralized immediately and the third took off, scampering frantic as a ferret. As the Stryker he was riding crunched to a stop, Dan was out and running before the ramp grounded. Thirty-six years old, with trick knees and a toting a combat load on his blue-collar back, Big Danny ran that young man down from behind and flattened him with a flying tackle.

After that, the grunts called him "Batman."

"Yep, that's me," Danny would grin, "keepin' the streets of Mosul safe for citizens."

Both our ears rang, Danny's and mine. No one seemed to believe it.

Danny was trying to get his concussion treated, but the VA made him wait until his claim was resolved, while his HMO insisted that he pay immediately for his MRI because his combat concussion was a "pre-existing condition." He was pinned between an actuarial rock and a government-funded hard place.

As for me, I was just trying to figure out why my head made the booming sounds sometimes. It hadn't used to. My board-certified, Poly Clinic internist said it was my heartbeat, but the boom was arrhythmic and besides, it didn't match the pulse in my neck. Checking for a pulse is in the Soldier's Manual of Common Tasks. Given enough live practice, most anyone can get pretty good at it.

The VA doctor said it was congestion rumbling in my Eustachian tubes, but my head wasn't congested. It was just noisy, between bilateral tinnitis and the weird booming. Usually, the booming was slow and hiccupy, like an idling Harley with one fouled plug. It came from inside and below my right ear.

One day, when I woke up hard to it rattling fast as a snare drum roll, I checked my pulse. It was 72 bpm, about normal for me. If it wasn't my pulse making the noise, then whose was it?

"Flanders came back and fell in the bottle pretty hard," Danny told me. "How's Russ doing?"

"Pretty sketchy, but he's working.

"I keep telling him about counseling, but he doesn't really want to talk about it," I said. "Can't really blame him."

Russ, the gunner on my team, feared the VA. Russ's big brother Bernard served as a medic with 173rd Parachute Infantry Regiment in the early days of the war (it was a *war*—right?) and came back from that experience a profoundly altered young man. He ended up service-connected at 80 percent disabled by PTSD and about 40 percent more disabled by his well-intended treatment.

Math is hard with TBI, multiplied by PTSD cubed over unemployment, carry the two.

Russ and Bernard's childhood friend and motocross buddy died in northern Iraq, throat-shot and gouting out his blood while Bernard cradled his head and watched the incandescent panic in his eyes gutter and fail. Bernard redeployed to exchange his Combat Medical Badge for a tongue stud and to subsist on a cocktail of government drugs and quarts of beer and maybe a dozen hours of hard-medicated sleep in a good week.

As a kid watching his grandpa die in an Old Soldiers' Home, Russ silently vowed never to end that way. Smoking out back of my Christmas party that year, Russ had been shivering pretty hard. I let it go, but someone we didn't know kept asking him if he wanted a jacket or something.

"Nah, it's alright," Russ finally told him. "I just shake like a Chihuahua all the time."

But I never saw him do it before that first machine gun dance, when he chopped up that guy in the parking lot.

Russ came back and transferred to a Special Forces company in the Guard, then got out and went to the police academy. He remained quiet, sensible, and forbearing in his commonsense way. What he really lived for was a good bar fight, gunning his cruiser solo up the road to back up the outnumbered cops in the next rural township.

I think Russ privately believed that if he just didn't acknowledge any demons, they would shrivel up and die instead of growing stronger in the dark places he banished them to. That if he just kept working quietly along, all the toxins would leach into the soil of his soul, and never poison his future. Sponged up by some kind of spiritual liver.

"Seems like everybody's having some kind of problems," Danny said. Then he smiled. "Well, everybody except Sergeant Doog."

Bronze Star Medal safely vested, Doog had retired to SCUBA dive in Hawaii.

I smiled back, but it was a bent kind of smile. "I heard what you meant—'everybody' as in 'all the team guys.'"

Our detachment had deployed at a strength of 13 soldiers, and received one replacement in theater. Nine of us served on tactical teams, attached to maneuver units at battalion/squadron level and supporting them at company/troop level.

Of the nine team guys, at least four that we could account for were under psychological treatment: Danny, Beaux, Will and me.

My gunner Russ held out because he was afraid he'd end up like his brother, and my driver Will was shot but was getting along okay, selling used cars.

From the rear D, two guys were diagnosed with "full-blown" PTSD: little Billy, who rotated through two tac teams; and Brian, whose R&R was his new wife's funeral after she was roasted alive in a Lynnwood apartment fire while he was cranking propaganda flyers through a risograph and setting up leaflet drops over Mosul.

"You and your wife getting along okay?" Danny's smile was as good-humored and skeptical as his eyes were exhausted.

"Not so much," I said. "She's been sleeping on the couch."

Dan smiled. "I know what you mean. Regina got really sick of me waking up suddenly."

"You mean when you kind of jerk awake?," I asked.

"Yeah. My PCP says those are some kind of convulsions."

"Shit, really? I thought…"

I didn't really know what I thought, but good Christ, was I relieved. Was I a unique head case? Maybe so—but if Big Danny and I lived in similar, self-mobilized rubber rooms, I was something other than alone.

It was so easy to problem-solve over there: don't feel well? Hydrate. Sleep if you can. Prep for missions. Go on missions. Eat a little. Hydrate.

Sleep.

Can't sleep? Exercise. Hydrate again. Try to sleep (good luck with that).

The army was dismissive about soldiers' issues. It was a game of macho points that we all played. "Sounds like a personal problem" was the standard answer, translated as: "We're serious people here. This is life and death.

"Take your damn whining somewhere else."

Any problems more complicated than eating, sleeping, hydrating and mission prep could be saved until you got home. It's a savings plan for personal problems that pays you back with interest, compounded hourly.

For the record, I didn't know what "full-blown PTSD" actually was.

My VA counselor confirmed that I had it. The VA claim reviewer remained unconvinced. Official sources agreed that it was actually a physical phenomenon, but it seemed like it must just be all in my head—even if my head felt empty, and even when everything hurt. A psychosomatic will o' the wisp. Postwar-partum depression.

The Congress of the United States of America agreed with the President of the United States of America that the waning stages of major overseas combat commitments were a fine time to cut funding to the VA; specifically to defund PTSD treatment centers and axe major studies of traumatic brain injury, such as a soldier might receive from experiencing an IED or two.

Or six.

Everyone agreed to agree that PTSD is no kind of weakness, but allowing pain to become an obstacle to performance is a soldier's *definition* of weakness. Another cliché, from an institution rife with them: "Pain is weakness leaving the body."

You could hardly blame our government for not wanting to namby-pamby a bunch of weak and broken former soldiers. In a down economy, what kind of return on investment would that bring?

Were we just squishy weekend warriors then, place-holding for the active guys? After all, don't real soldiers get up and go again, until they retire or come back dead?

Some of the smartest, strongest, most capable soldiers I've met served in that detachment. Before we ever met each other, Danny had toted a SAW through Somalia as a lance corporal on a Special Boats team; Myron had operated Patriots during Desert Storm; Cal had honchoed a PSYOP team in Bosnia; I'd spent a year on Korea's DMZ.

We had two firefighters, a semi-pro football player and a mat-sparring drug investigator who could bench press economy cars. Our commander helped write the doctrine for psychological operations. We all had campaign medals from somewhere else before we deployed to Iraq. Polite Reservists, we secretly imagined that we just might be pretty badass.

We built an FM radio station, ran air drops, published a newspaper, broadcast messages on loudspeakers, contracted and erected billboards, patrolled mounted and kicked in doors, patrolled dismounted and shook endless unwashed hands, drank gallons of *chai* and skinfuls of goat's milk. We ran hundreds of assaults and suspect detentions and overwatches and cordon searches with the infantry and cavalry we supported.

When the 1st of the 25th Stryker Brigade Combat Team received a Valorous Unit Award, its exceptional employment of psychological operations was called out in the award text. The brigade's entire psychological operations output was produced by seventeen Reservists from Tactical PYOP Detachment 1290.

We took no weenies: every man and woman SOF-certified on their PT and marksmanship, road marches and land navigation.

…no dummies: every soldier in the detachment had college. More than half of us were degreed once or twice.

…and no cowards: every team guy was a "three-time loser" who had enlisted, petitioned to join a team, and volunteered to deploy.

When Tactical PSYOP Detachment 1290 finished up our tour, brigade commander COL Brown called our efforts "the most effective use of PSYOP since Operation Iraqi Freedom began."

Then he walked the line and shook our hands, hung identical Army Commendation medals from all of our shirts with bulldog clips, then pinned a Bronze Star each onto CPT Parrish and Doog.

After a public affairs specialist snapped pictures, we stayed locked up at parade rest in the sun, waiting for a female staff puke to come along and police up all the pretty ARCOMs into a paper sack. Impatient with the ritual, I had already pocketed mine, broken formation and turned away in disgust by the time she came by to collect it.

The Badge of Military Merit, a "Figure of a Heart in Purple Cloth or Silk edged with narrow Lace or Binding" was devised by Gen. George Washington for the twin purposes of inspiring valor and distracting soldiers from their conspicuous lack of pay envelopes. By policy, the Badge was awarded to enlisted troops exclusively for, as Napoleon Bonaparte would shortly observe, "A soldier will fight long and hard for a bit of colored ribbon."

At the urging of Gen. John J. "Blackjack" Pershing, our original "bit of colored ribbon" was carried forward in 1932 when, in commemoration of the bicentennial of Washington's birth and of his democratic ideals, army chief of staff Gen. Douglas MacArthur created the Purple Heart Medal for meritorious service.

The Bronze Star Medal was created 12 years later, by executive order of President Franklin D. Roosevelt, to recognize "heroic or meritorious achievement or service" by soldiers in wartime. Its purpose was straightforward: to recognize fighting American grunts. Gen. George C. Marshall was blunt in describing the target demographic:

> *The fact that the ground troops, Infantry in particular, lead miserable lives of extreme discomfort and are the ones who must close in personal combat with the enemy, makes the maintenance of their morale of great importance. The award of the Air Medal has had an adverse reaction on the ground troops, particularly the Infantry Riflemen who are now suffering the heaviest losses, air or ground, in the Army, and enduring the greatest hardships.*

Few men are Bonapartes; even fewer are Marshalls. During OIF[38], captains collected Bronze Stars for getting lost in scary neighborhoods without an armored cavalry regiment at their back and staff colonels were insulted by any medal short of a Legion of Merit, but a Bronze Star often cost plain ground troopers an arm and a leg.

They were awarded on a relentless quota system that required wresting one from the careerist clutches of higher-ups. To win at office politics, you have to hang around the office, but my team had spent our tour a hundred miles from the flagpole. I did my guys a disservice by running missions instead of running interference up the chain of command, and their extraordinary service earned them ordinary accolades.

The more things change, the more they remain the same. The very first Purple Heart was awarded moments after its creation by Gen. MacArthur… to Gen. MacArthur.

In my front pocket, next to a Benchmade folding knife, rode a chrome Zippo with the shiny enameled crests I'd epoxied on before we deployed. On one side, the modest white crest of 12th PSYOP Battalion read *MUTATIO ANIMI* ("to change the spirit"). On the other side, the flashy chess knight of our regimental crest was surrounded by laurels and a green banner bearing the legend "PERSUADE CHANGE INFLUENCE."

---

[38] Operation Iraqi Freedom.

While we lurked in the dim, plywood transient barracks, waiting on a C130 to Kuwait, I slipped my lighter into Russ's duffel bag along with the green ribbon representing his "thanks for playing" award.

Hear O Israel, as God is my witness, I will smoke no more forever.

This is stupid, I thought, resolving to get up immediately and take action. *It's a holiday, for fuck's sake. A celebration.*

I was huddled down between the queen-size bed and Melanie's cherry dresser, tucked into a fetal squish halfway under one of the nightstands I once built from a few sweet, hoarded Peruvian walnut boards and two expensive, wany-edged, spalted maple slabs. They were gorgeous little pieces if I say so myself, but they sure made lousy bunkers. Fourth of July barrages arced smoke and lights over Lake Washington, each flash followed by a concussive detonation and an inexplicable whimpering sound.

But sergeants never run from our bogeymen. Consider the sergeants of the field, how they lead from the front: they neither whimper nor cower, yet I tell you, even Rumsfeld in his glory was not arrayed like one of these. I lowered my forearms away from my ears and stood, flinching only a little at the lights and explosions.

The time had come to advance to the rear. I fell back to the kitchen area in a tactical withdrawal to rest and refit. There I reloaded with two hydrocodones stolen from Mel's oral surgery leftovers, and refueled on four or five quick beers from the fridge door.

Thus mission-prepped, I maneuvered decisively to the television set and turned it up so loud I couldn't hear anything over Jon Stewart deconstructing the news.

Dominating my battle space, I had retaken the house.

"What the hell is going on in here?," Melanie yelled, three times until I heard her and turned around, squinting and grinning.

"Nothin', darlin'." I grinned even wider, showing teeth like a naked skull. "Everything is *fine!*"

"I'm worried about your use of drugs and alcohol," Björn said at our next session a week later.

"Oh, I've been pretty good," I told him very seriously. "That was an anomaly."

"And the other times you told me about a couple of weeks ago, when you drank yourself to sleep—were those 'anomalies,' too?"

"Absolutely."

My deal with God and Fate and karma was this: if I took care of my guys, I'd be alright. Even if I got blown to scraps, I'd be alright.

I doubt I'll ever learn what heaven is, but Hell is knowing you didn't do all you could. I was lucky, and they came home with all their pieces attached, able to work and live and love, and only one bullet hole between them. It was more grace than I deserved, though less than they earned.

Thank You, Lord.

Four months after I started sessions with Björn and three months after I started to take Welbutrin, I lived a watershed day: it didn't feel too cold, and I wasn't too worried about folks "looking at me." When I ventured out of the house, people seemed friendly enough.

It wasn't such a fearful world when I faced it and moved in it, but I took baby steps nonetheless: into gun shops and hardware stores, surplus outlets and veterans' museums where dey speaka my language. I was polite and quiet, and they were carefully solicitous, and it all worked pretty well except for the time I got on an articulated express bus and sat in the seat over the mid-body hinge.

Every few hundred feet when it boomed and heaved up vertically, I was dead sure we'd run over an IED. It wasn't forebrain knowledge—it was my ass taking control. My ass stubbornly insisted on me saving it, whether I took an interest in the project or not.

At our sessions, Björn would remind me not to kill myself. He made solid arguments, but my give-a-shit factor was too low to respect the logic.

So we made a deal on his insistence: I was not allowed to kill myself without calling him first.

It wasn't a deal that Melanie had thought to make.

There is honor or dishonor in every small choice. Taking care of those around you: there is honor. But back home, no one needed my strong-arm care. Other than a few determined moon bats and war pushers, lives proceeded as though nothing out of the ordinary had occurred. Here in our uneasy peace, where could anyone find honor? And how could I keep from shrieking out the things that were too heavy to carry, unloading them on every passing citizen?

"Use your anger," Björn advised, "it's your fuel."

Where was that fuel driving me?

I didn't know who to be angry at. There were no ROE[39]. Moral complexity and ambiguity are interesting ivory tower games, but those sophomoric discussions evaporated in the face of life or death decision-making faster than piss bottle splatter off a Mosul cabbie's windshield. Combat stakes were too high and evaluated too quickly to allow the academic luxury of inventorying pinheaded angels.

Taking the home folks' problems seriously had become a tad difficult for me. Eventually I relearned that blaring, "I don't give a shit about your petty little problems!" was not the best way

---

[39] Rules Of Engagement. Like nearly all military acronyms, ROE can be used as a noun or verb; tenses and plurals are casual.

to rebuild trust and confidence with one's spouse, but that knowledge came back to me too late to explain it to Mel.

How do you un-ring the alarum bells of war? It would be easier to sanctify a whorehouse. Maybe that's why the epithet for non-combat troops is "cherries."

I wondered if the rear-echelon frat boys who chopped down our cherry tree would ever have the sack to admit to it.

Lying on the bed one evening, listening to the hiss and splash while waiting for Melanie to come out of shower, I looked up to find myself surrounded by cats.

Framed like a chromed Degas, Melanie smiled from behind the glass. "You're loved. You know that."

I pointed out the bed rats, one by one: Hunter, Minnie, Big Ears.

"Yes," she said, "they love you."

I pointed at her.

"Yes." She smiled. "Me, too. I love you. You're loved by all of us."

I put my head back on the pillow, looked up at the ceiling. Minnie nuzzled my hand, and I stroked her soft bat ears. Mel was preparing to leave me soon, or more accurately to push me out of her life. Graduating from pushing out of my hugs to pushing out of our marriage, she had found herself a fellow adventurer whom she was not quite ready to reveal. I would find all of this out very soon.

She put up with me for over a year after I redeployed, then she put me out. Can't blame her. My temper and spookiness must have been a trial. Trying to explain it to her hadn't gone over very well.

"I'm glad you're seeing a counselor," she answered every time, "but I don't really want to hear about it."

In the meantime, she found some counseling—succor, anyway—for herself. One afternoon in what was once our kitchen, Melanie re-confirmed that I would give insulin shots and thyroid medication to her aging cats when she went with our friends on the Hood-To-Coast, a 196-mile relay we had used to run together.

"Sure." I smiled curiously at her. "I said I would, so I will."

Then she asked if I would kitty-sit over the holidays.

"Holidays?," I said. "Why? Are you visiting Ma?"

"I'm going to Wyoming for Thanksgiving."

I looked at her carefully for a moment, perhaps not realizing how high my eyebrows were climbing.

"Meeting the parents, are we?"

Silence from her.

"Mel, are you sleeping with this guy?"

More silence.

Then, "What does it matter?"

How could I expect Melanie to understand what I didn't understand myself until I saw it?

She was a horrible PITA, but she had been, once upon a time, brave and rippingly honest. She tried—or anyway, seemed to try—to put up with my bubbling emotional stew. Still, I found it hard to take her ending every conversation by saying "Let's just not talk anymore," and turning up the radio for another East Coast social lecture.

I wondered when she started seeing him, when she started thinking about seeing him—or just seeing someone, anyone. I wondered whether she originally formed the concept with a particular man in mind, or whether any man would do so long as he met certain criteria, such as not being me.

I wondered whether she started seeing him while I was overseas, launching intercontinental ballistic love notes at her. Maybe her e-mailed replies were *pro forma*; she was supporting the troops with digital care packages but tying no yellow ribbons. I guessed that it didn't matter.

It sure felt like it mattered.

I would miss Melanie, but I had been missing her for some time by then, even when she was right beside me. It may have been what my first wife meant when she talked about that "homesick at home" feeling.

Practice had not improved me.

I had always believed you are not what you eat, and you're not who you think you are inside. You are nothing more than what you do. When you help, you are kind; when you steal, you're a thief. Killing makes you a killer.

These are simple truths.

The road to Hell is not, I'm told, paved by your actions. Hell is failing your better nature by falling short of your good intentions. Hell is hearing the whisper that your limitations are far more profound than you ever believed, there in your secret heart of hearts where you see yourself in terms of possibilities. Self-actualizing mediocrity: that way lies Hell.

But I never believed it. I always thought you could work your way, bribe your way or fight your way out of Hell by your deeds—or condemn yourself the same way. Jesus was a known optimist, and I've never trusted the promise of unearned grace.

Left me in a bit of a bind, that did.

I was no hero, not on my best day. It never mattered how fast I could run, how far I could ruck, how much I could bench. It wasn't about being the first guy up or the last to the sack, carrying the most gear, volunteering for dirty duty, or running the highest OPTEMPO. It wasn't even about whether I backed down under fire, or held onto the will to direct my men.

I was never going to be "that guy," the Silver Star winner, the hero of the day. Never a poster boy and not a role model, either. Maybe not, on balance, even one of the good guys. Surely not the jaunty champion on the billboard; just the soldier next door. Another guy who never quite lived up to his own ideal, who slid through a mid-life reckoning and straight into not defeat, but a kind of resignation.

You are what you do, and I hadn't done much. Yet there I found myself ("no shit, there I was...," as all war stories and some true stories start), lying across the marital bed for one of the last times, surrounded by a passel of furballs who didn't give a rip about my résumé.

All cats seem to possess their own flavor of PTSD. It's kind of a kitty birthright, so naturally I went easy around them and we all got along. They only wanted a stroke or a scritch, and for me not to move too fast. They were happy to be happy.

There are lessons there.

My dress uniform has thirteen little ribbons on it now, and some of them mean something. Any army vet can read that blouse and tell a lot about where I've been and what I've done— in the army. But nothing in my personnel file documents all that went between being a big-eyed private learning his way and a tired old staff sergeant with a few things to teach the real heroes: those soldiers marching bravely into their unknown futures. All the messy life that happened between those regimented green bookends is mine to keep, or to share. The army has had her portion.

The ribbons don't define me, and ten months of my life is hardly a summary. Hundreds of thousands of us went to Iraq, most got through it and came back, and everyone dealt with some fallout.

Even you.

Every soldier's family went through pain, loss and change, even those whose soldiers are visibly unwounded.

Every Reservist and every Guardsman still under contract faces the prospect of going again and again, every time this country calls until they are physically unable to come to the line. And every citizen pays the tab.

But it doesn't define them, either.

The soldiers in your neighborhood are more than their "killer stripes," more than their PT scores and rifle badges and combat patches and campaign medals and decorations. They are more than their war stories, although many of them tell better'n average war stories if you know how to listen.

They are part of your neighborhood, part of your PTSA, part of your corporation, part of the soul of your city. When they're not drilling or training or fighting your wars, you'll find them building your community alongside you.

My friends, my daughter, my neighbors cared for me. Completely defying my pragmatic philosophy, they believed that I was more than what I did. They believed that I embodied more than the various chits and markers pinned to the 46-Regular blouse hanging in the guest closet, seven hangers and two decades down the rack from the 39-Long issued to me in 1983.

I'll keep those colored bits of ribbon, though.

Surely I'll never throw them over the fence to protest a political administration: let our leaders earn their own medals. Let them go, and lead from the front in the ancient tradition of warrior kings, and become worthy to ponder war.

As for my own small ribbons, they are not the sum of me, but—like my fellow soldiers, living and dead, active and reserve—they are part of me.

Always.

I was proud to be the soldier I had been since '83,

when I joined to pay for college like my brothers before me.

I was proud to serve my country and to be a fine Marine,

but pride cannot protect me from the things that I have seen.

—Richard Shindell, *Things That I Have Seen*

GREEN FLASH

*My beloved spake, and said unto me, Rise up, my love, my
fair one, and come away. For lo, the winter is past, the rain is
over and gone;*

*The flowers appear on the earth; the time of the singing
of birds is come, and the song of the turtle is heard in our
land;*

—Song of Solomon, 2:10-11

It was just a three-hour business drone from Seattle to
Portland. Then Tacoma's commuter traffic crunched over my
patience and left it bleeding by the Jersey barriers of Interstate
Five. I broke right and peeled off west out Highway 16 toward
water, peace and two-lane solutions.

Out past Gig Harbor sits a seafood 'n' ice cream pizza
emporium. Nobody in his right mind passes up a fried
Hoodsport oyster burger washed down with fork-thick chocolate
malt, and I don't, either.

Waddling back out to my new R1200S (aka "Black
Betty") after lunch, I waved at the ST1300 rider I had waved at

on the way in, but he was still nattering into his cell phone. My cell phone, which doesn't work on good roads or sunny days, was tucked into my tank bag.

BMW makes hella expensive bike luggage and their zipper pulls are crap, but they're stubbornly waterproof, fit close and look sharp as a Nazi officer's coat. Thanks to the joys of employee discounting, my Betty sported a tail bag to match. And rocker cover guards, six-inch rear wheel, Swedish shocks, smoked screen, monoposto cover and a booming carbon-ti stinger in place of the stock baboon's arsehole.

As a friend says, "shop to ride, ride to shop."

Black Betty's final touch is black "Speed" wheels, which the inscrutable Bavarians refuse to sell on their *schwarzer* "S" bikes. Betty's stock silver wheels had been swapped onto a candy cane 12S and delivered south to ferry a spiky but juicy girl around San Francisco.

Onward, then, west along where SR 302 curves two sweet lanes around Case Inlet's northern reach, past the road leading to Penrose Point State Park. Twenty years ago in that park, I stood and bawled into the stony salt beach for my one true Catholic girl, cloistered into the nearby women's penitentiary at Purdy where she still haunts a cell today.

I didn't stop this time. The freshly paved road was too curvaceously inviting for patricidal reminiscences.

So there I was, burbling lively along on a spankin' new bike, bound for my first reading of new material at a major bookstore and the first long ride with my self-selected "number one groupie." Great roads rushed up to meet me like old friends returned, bathed in northwest sun (another old friend returned from seasons away). Chilly salt air bit my nose and a Gerbing electric liner gently toasted my chest. Freshly debrided Metzeler Sportecs stuck to the road like bandages on a wet scab.

Life is pretty good, I thought. Wandering south on a congenial errand, a couple hours overdue with a pretty girl waiting... *d'oh!*

IDIOT BOY!

I pulled over and left a *mea culpa* on Pretty Girl's cell phone, then beat it down State Route 3, past Hartstene Island's beachcombing shacks and the Squaxin Island rez and across the base of the rain forest peninsula through Shelton. From Isabella Lake I took the 101 into Olympia the back way. Mandatory slabbing to Portland wasn't excuse enough to divert out to Cooper Point and drain beers with friends, so I droned south, cheerfully waving at big women on Harleys.

On Broadway in downtown Portland, the Marriott's doorkid was explaining their valet motorcycle parking ("a couple of our guys have endorsements"), when someone seized me from behind and I nearly leapt out of my leathers. I hate getting jumped from behind, but the Lord loves a grinning girl and so do I.

Pretty Girl had been pounding on her laptop in Peet's coffee shop when she detected the gentle murmur of Betty's Akrapovic exhaust fracturing windows up and down the street. The BMW catalog calls it a "sport silencer," which is half-true. I am not a nice man, but I know what makes me happy: black bikes, blacktop, and black leathers. And Pretty Girl, who isn't big enough to be a Harley girl yet.

A weekend in Oregon with a delightful woman, a reading, then a spring ride to the coast.

How bad could that be?

En route to my reading the next day, Pretty Girl took a call from Seattle's Moto International shop. She snapped her phone shut, looking defeated. Seems her beloved Moto Guzzi Mille GT hadn't just spun a crank bearing. "Sal" would require a new camshaft, too. Pretty Girl wordlessly pointed at a Pearl District dessert shop. Playing my first responder role, I swept her in for dark chocolate and espresso, patted her hand and congratulated her on her foresight in procuring a backup bike.

A few quality ringers, including my undeservedly loyal mother, attended my reading at Powell's City of Books the next evening. It went well. We celebrated at Kelly's Olympian, the third-oldest bar in Portland. The Oly featured a menagerie of shiny old motorcycles, a tap line of micro-brewed inspiration and kick-ass onion rings.

The second morning, we checked out and blasted down Canyon Boulevard. Pretty Girl felt slightly less bereft of her Guzzi once she pulled her very first wheelie on her Tweety-yellow 2002 BMW F650GS. Such a sparkly stoplight smile I never saw before.

Two miles later, a 20-something dude pulled up and ogled Black Betty's Öhlins-spangled legs. "Can that bike wheelie?"

"With all this luggage on?," I said. "You're nuts!"

He shrugged and grinned.

It's common knowledge that shafties won't wheelie. Figuring to show my date a for-real wheelstand, I quit caressing Betty's mighty throttle bodies and gave them a heavy grope.

The rangy black bitch was bellowing and stretching toward heaven when I fat-toed her into neutral and she crashed down faster than the walls of Jericho at a bugle recital.

Uff da!

The brochure never mentioned a fully interactive crotch-tank interface. Well, it probably wouldn't hurt unless I tried to walk, or breathe, or something. So impressive to the new girlfriend...

Out of McMinnville we headed north toward Yamhill, then meandered west along Panther Creek, past grassy Meadow Lake reservoir on a road that jukes bluesy through the Coast Range, keeping time to the syncopated curves of the Nestucca River. Fissured and crumbled, graveled and frost-heaved, that road jerks and slashes through the trees like a wino with a chainsaw. I reined Black Betty in, trying to be sociable.

After 20 minutes, Pretty Girl putted up at a stop and told me to quit dawdling and "go have some fun." The heavens opened, and choral music issued forth. Who raises such women—and why hadn't I meet one years ago?

When I realized I could also write this trip off my taxes, I suddenly understood the angelic choir. Obviously, I had died and been delivered to the wrong address.

Not once did Betty put a wide black wheel wrong. The 2007 R1200S is sure-footed like a mountain-bred mustang. Two big slugs squeezing 12.5:1 compression, four spark plugs, cams in the heads, about fifty pounds porkier than my old Duc but packing fifty extra horsepower and room to store my legs. Greatest old man's touring bike *evah*.

We were touching 90 on a short straight when the road zagged left and turned to muddy gravel.

Oy vey! What a terrible dirt bike!

Eight minutes later, Pretty Girl zipped past with a big wave, backed it into the next corner all crossed up and dragging her Givi saddlebag, then disappeared up the road while I tippy-toed effetely around potholes with trembling clip-ons.

Once back on hardtop, we barrel-assed into Beaver and soared north on the open coast highway. Paying her back a little, I waved and let Betty out to gallop the long sweepers. Pausing for a short discussion about endurance, we backtracked to a scenic loop I've been bypassing for years. From an overlook 200 feet above the booming surf, we envied the parasailers frolicking on afternoon thermals.

"Hold me for a minute?," she said. "I'm a little cold."

Pretty Girl's Gerbing had died without a whimper somewhere along the forest road, leaving her with two unheated layers, under a mesh jacket, in early spring, on the clammy coast. With my Heat-Troller cranked up to "magma" and my heated grips on "fricassee," I was chilly myself. We swapped Heat-Trollers, but her jacket was fried. Adding layers helped little.

As the sun fell, the temperature dropped from the low 60s into the 50s, then into the high 40s. Sunshine turned to mist and graduated to squalls.

"Want to ride Betty?," I said. "She's got heated grips."

"Don't want to ride an unfamiliar bike when I'm not on my game. My ruler's a couple inches short right now."

What man would admit to that?

I had nothin'. They say the true test for a couple is putting up a tent together in the rain. We were sodden with all the frustration, cold and fatigue—just no tent. This was a forced march, not a dance. We trudged on, private thoughts giving way to mindless endurance.

At Fresh Seafood NW in Tillamook, rubber-booted fishermen toted in dripping string bags of cold-water oysters and Dungeness crabs from rusty Chevy pickups. When we pulled in, the stouthearted proprietress took one look at Pretty Girl and unclosed her lunch counter.

Bustling purposefully, Kari scooped us a bucket of meaty white chowder, boiled up fresh coffee and told us to ignore closing time. Hands wrapped onto steaming cups, we slurped hot, salty fluids until we felt approximately human. Then, sighing, we clumped back out into the cold, alone beside each other in the gravel parking lot.

"I'm really having a good time." ...*compared to a Vise-Grip pedicure.*

"Are you sure?" *Are you off your meds?*

Her face was windburnt and her hair was snarled, but her smile was true clear up to the eyes.

I was a mother hen as a sergeant, but as a rider I make a lousy babysitter. I don't do group rides; I'm impatient with manufactured "biker" events and my buddies are not riding buddies. My first modification to a new bike is to unbolt the passenger pegs, put them in a box, and lose the box. The motorcycle is for me.

But here was this girl, pretty and brave, riding her own and gutting it out. A puzzler.

At stop after stop, I plied Pretty Girl with every possible form of warmth, waiting for the first little whine to breach her dam of resolve. All I heard was, "I'm OK.

"Just hold me for a minute."

On we slogged as the road unreeled, slow and cold. Shadows inveigled our highway down into their dead embrace. Ghosts darted from corners. But we were on our bikes, going through it together.

We still had two hours separating us from a warm bed in Gearhart when we pulled off at Wheeler to watch the sunset. Our chances looked worse with every stop, but hypothermia is not indefinitely negotiable. I curled my arm around her shoulders, faced west and held on until she stopped bucking with shivers.

"My grandfather told me," Pretty Girl said, teeth chattering, "if you watch the sunset just when it disappears below the horizon, you can see an afterglow.

"It's called the 'Green Flash'."

"Sounds like a comic book hero," I said, being sensitive like that.

"Grandpa was my hero." *Oh. Nice one, Lewis.*

"Sometimes you remind me of him." *Oh...*

I pulled Pretty Girl inside my jacket and we watched the flaming slick of sun drizzle over the edge of the world. Seabirds cruised low over the salt marsh, and bulrushes rustled across the estuary where the Nehalem River tiptoes in to slip between the sheets of the sea.

I looked into my riding partner's face. Her blue eyes flashed green just as the last orange fire flared out of the sky and branded the image of her smile into my mind.

Standing with her in the dark, I started believing we could make it.

Cold and dark it was when we finally fumbled our way to Mom's "beach cabin," a faded former real estate office situated on a quiet Gearhart street that has gentrified alarmingly in every direction.

We proudly parked our bikes in the only remaining all-grass driveway on the block, turned on the water, wrestled the door locks open and were only mildly perturbed when we couldn't get the lights to come on or the furnace fan to run. I did manage to get the burners on the gas range going.

"It's okay," said Pretty Girl. "We'll go get some pie and heat it up, and it'll make everything smell like home, and get us nice and warm."

She may have noticed the ol' cabin was a touch musty.

Piling two-up onto the mini-Beemer because it still had its rear pegs, we repaired to the Seaside Safeway for frozen cherry pie and some light bulbs to replace the ones that mysteriously popped every time a switch was thrown, with a fistful of candles and a box of stick matches for backup. When we got back, we discovered the gas oven wouldn't fire up, either. That pie would need to go into a freezer, but I was afraid to crack open the crypt-silent fridge.

Sigh.

Pretty Girl shook out some sheets, and they exploded with bird dust and seeds. Quietly, she went into the front room and sat down on my aunt's old leather couch with a blank look.

1930s USN-surplus cots awaited us, sort of like a wooden rack featuring a hammock crossed with a straitjacket. Any bed beats no bed after a good, long, cold day. Pretty Girl crawled gratefully into the nearest one, and stiffened up.

"It's… wet."

I lunged for the spare sheets. They were damp, too.

Please, God, don't let her cry. I'd been telling Pretty Girl about the family cabin practically since we had met—how we used to pick blackberries in the summer, pull dinners of mussels off the rocks, play in the tide pools, and catch crabs by hand in the brackish river. She knew how important that place was to me.

"It's always like this," I told her, trying to remember if it was.

"Hey," she said, reaching out a hand. "Why don't you get in here and warm me up?"

Well, a few more bars of angel music wouldn't hurt anyone.

The sheets were dry and warm when we woke up, lending credibility to hypothermia guidance dimly remembered from my 70s-edition Boy Scout Manual. I turned on all four range burners and opened both doors to let the cabin hiss out vapor like a Mt. Saint Helens steam fissure, while Pretty Girl rummaged through her gear and came up with a multi-meter.

"You carry a volt/ohm meter everywhere you ride?"

She looked at me like I'd just jammed my thumb in my nose. "Hel-*lo!*

"Uh, Guzzi owner…?"

Oh. Yeah. Italian bikes are reliably interesting, which is not the same as reliable.

At the box, I figured out that we had one leg of power out. The power company emergency line had a crew dispatched within a few hours to put it straight, and we enjoyed one halfway warm and better-lit night before heading south along the coast, toward closer approximations of home. I yanked off the road reflexively when we got to the Tillamook crab shack.

"Nice to see you!," Kari chirped, setting up a fresh pot.

Gurgling full of warm seafood, we struck south down the 101 past Beaver through Hebo, Cloverdale and Neskowin, over the summit past Otis to Neotsu and on through Lincoln City before turning east on SR 229. That road gambols south over the Euchre Mountain through Siletz before banging broadside into the 20.

Between Chitwood and Blodgett, Highway 20 is a veritable research library of smooth sweepers. It's abysmally mired in Airstreams and Winnebagos every weekend, but this was a Monday. The biggest blockade we saw was a horde of touring bikes led by a BMW R1150RT, painted a light enough shade that I performance-tested my ABS before realizing it wasn't piloted by a cop. We promptly returned to the kind of frisky behavior that resulted in my 190/50 getting cleanly scrubbed right out to the sidewalls. Pretty Girl and her Tweety weren't wasting any time (or lane space) either.

"You know you're on knobbies, right?," I asked at a sunglasses stop in Philomath, after our road's interest had broadened from the wiry technical toward the fatly scenic.

"It's a light bike," Pretty Girl said, grinning. I used to be amazed by people whose smiles could light up a room. Now I'd met one who could illuminate a rural highway.

She looked at me for a minute. "When we get to the junction—"

"I'll head north up the 99 from here," I said. I had work to do. In Seattle as in many places, the week starts on Tuesday at motorcycle shops.

"Yeah," she said with a shy kind of smile that was maybe a little bit sad, "if it's okay with you, I'm just going to pretend you're on an errand, and you'll be back in a little while."

It was pretty close to true, and she was pretty close to me, so I reached out and hugged that pretty girl, as Arlo Guthrie might say, "once more... with *feelin'*."

Then she grinned, and flipped her visor down, and gassed that little Beemer up the highway. I rode in formation with her until the overpass at Corvallis, where I peeled off the exit and turned left, and Pretty Girl continued on to hit I-5 south at Albany.

On the overpass, I looked out to my right and watched her go. With golden fingers of sunset ricocheting lightning off her helmet as she burned east on her brave little bike, she shone like a brand new key.

PUPPERS

They're some of the biggest dogs in the world. Pretty Wife has wanted one for 20 years, but it's never been the right time. It'll never be the right time, but what could it hurt to look?

The Craigslist picture was unprepossessing—a sad puppy with a blotchy gray coat sat staring dull-eyed at the floor—but his story tugged at us. The woman who placed the ad took in his dam and him from the police when he was one week old, sole survivor of his litter. At nine weeks, his puppy belly was distended and his spine stuck out like Nessie's back plates.

"He doesn't look too good," I said.

"I never wanted a merle," Pretty Wife replied.

We saddled up and drove straight there. It was only a three-hour round trip.

From the ten-foot fence in the yard, half a dozen Great Danes boomed at us like frantic foghorns, their voices trembling the glass in our little Toyota. On the lawn, the rescue woman stood with a pup trembling at her feet, ears back and eyes white around the edges. His tail was tucked so far under it tickled at his muzzle. He tiptoed with an uncertain wobble, hips thrust under his belly. A Great Dane, but maybe not The Greatest Dane.

We talked softly to him while we chatted with his rescue mum. He finally ventured off his special towel long enough to clump over on wrinkly puppy cankles and sniff at our faces. Pretty Wife stroked him a bit. I petted him once or twice, then he lurched into my shin and leaned on me until I picked him up and realized that an infant Great Dane is the size of a medium dog.

Trembling, he put his head under my chin and pushed into the warmth. He gave me a serious look, like he didn't know that puppies smell like buttered toast and baby toes.

"Well, we'd better go," said Pretty Wife, for the second or third time.

"Y'all think about it, okay? He likes you guys," said the rescue lady. "I have a good feeling about this."

Pretty Wife and I have a standing agreement, pan-situationally applied: it's my fault, but her responsibility. On the upshift from third to fourth, she said, "I don't think that's the puppy I've been waiting for.

"He was trembling and had his tail tucked the whole time we were there. 'Fearful' is a deal-breaker for me in a 200-lb. dog. Anyway, his conformation isn't great."

I watched the road. Crashing would be my fault. I shifted carefully into fifth.

"I always thought my Dane pup would be a blue or a black."

That puppy had just been cold, was all. He had character written all over his merly little schnozz. I would have said something, but I was squinting pretty hard through the rain, so I turned up the wipers instead.

"Oh, my gosh," said Pretty Wife. She looked closely at me for a moment. "Is he *your* puppy?"

I kept my eyes on the road where they belonged. For the next few days, Pretty Wife gently rationalized me into believing that it would be okay for me to have a puppy.

Me!

The prospect was terrifying. I like dogs about the way I like kids: thoroughly housebroken, preferably college-educated.

"His name is Tucker," I finally told her.

Five days later, we picked him up. In the interim, he'd grown almost an inch at the shoulder. All the way home, he shook, drooled, and startled at passing trucks, but he snuggled close and never whined once. The picture of him sitting on my lap that first day shows my entire right arm saturated with pup spit. His mien remained morbidly grave...

"I dunno," I told Pretty Wife. "Maybe 'Tucker' is short for 'Tail Tucker.'"

The next day, 90 minutes in advance of his first veterinary visit, Tucker launched a spray of mustard-yellow horror across our yard, the long white contents of which waved at me like alien tentacles freshly exploded from Sigourney Weaver's theretofore flawless belly. Tucker looked up at me uncertainly.

"Um ... good dog?"

Good Lord, I thought.

Opting for the Powell Doctrine, I scraped up and threw away a four-foot square of turf, bleached the ground underneath it, then bleached the garbage can. Pretty Wife had to restrain me from bleaching Tucker.

Once wormed, Tucker's coat brightened into shredded dark patches over a beautiful blue background, with snowy white paws and chest. Eyes brightening as fast as his coat, Tucker's appetite picked up and his energy soared into puppy overdrive.

Tucker started looking more like a dwarf weightlifter than a Lesser Dane. His bloated belly sleeked into his knobby frame and the lumps of his spine subsumed themselves between twin ridges of puppy muscle, ideal for gnawing bones and tugging on ropes.

"Maybe his name is 'Tugger'."

Tucker tentatively clumped around our living room on his snow-boot paws, wrinkling his forehead curiously at every new sight and smell, and retreating to my lap at every new sound.

Tucker groaned in his sleep like an old Labrador retriever. When it woke Pretty Wife up, I gently suggested to her that it was the sound of his bones stretching.

Three times a night for the first week, I got up and carried him from his puppy crate to the front door, escorting him out to execute the formalities. Now that he's down to once a night, I automatically wake up at 0300. When he finally sleeps through the night, I'll be proud as a new parent—and just as relieved. Right now, there's not enough coffee in the world, and he's growing so fast that if he doesn't start walking out the door on his own pretty soon, there won't be enough Advil, either.

Over the next few days, he burst right out of his shell. Tucker now prances around, trying to instigate doggie games with our old mix, Auggie. Tucker also finds himself an endless stock of shoes, papers and socks to steal and chew when we aren't looking. When he bounds across the living room, it sounds like a herd of elk stampeding through a dance studio.

Tucker's skinny worm of a tail—so poorly matched to his Frankenpup paws—now waves as cheerfully as a Frisco rainbow flag. He's no tail tucker! In fact, it may turn out to be a chore convincing him he's not the alpha male around here.

Auggie would prefer to believe that the interloper is, at worst, a temporary distraction. A practical dog, Auggie takes the good with the bad. After the first few days of copious treats to fend off his jealousy, Auggie's collar disappeared under furry rolls, gone to wherever it is that my belt hides when I'm wearing it.

After three days of yapping at Auggie with his chin on the ground and his lumpy hips waggling, Tucker finally got the old dog's attention by darting for his bone. There followed—in instantaneous order—a roar, a snap and a terrified shriek. Tucker rolled up into the corner by our bed, coiled tight as a potato bug and whimpering like a spun bearing. There wasn't a mark on him. Auggie had bitch-slapped him with the sides of his overgrown tusks.

It's become a regular game for them. Tails waving, they face off over a bone. Auggie hunkers over his treasure like a flatulent, overfed dragon with Tucker crouching low, pretending to hide in the grass while he yaps his fool head off. When Auggie finally roars and comes for him, Tucker skips away with a smile curved into his tail.

Today, Tucker baited Auggie into lunging completely off the bone pile. Then, while the old dog circled and sniffed, Tucker dashed in for the kill and emerged triumphantly with a mouthful of bones. Chuffing his jowls and wriggling his linguine tail, the pup loped over to his corner. All the way across the room, he watched Auggie out of the corner of his eye, bouncing like Muhammed Ali in the third round of a Liston bout.

Tucker is smart, he's brave and he's going to be about my size by late next year.

That old dog is in such trouble.

COAT OF MANY COLORS

That old Levis jacket, Chinese-made with American fade, had almost every unit patch I'd ever worn sewn onto the back.

Peacetime insignia were in full color: Second Infantry Division, my first assignment in Korea with E Battery (TAB), 25th Field Artillery; III Corps where I worked personnel security for the corps artillery, initiating nosy searches on battalion commanders of the type that are now warrantlessly routine for simple citizens; 24th Infantry Division (Mechanized) from my last peacetime, active duty stint with Charlie Battery, 1st of the 13th Field Artillery (Multiple Launch Rocket System).

Rounding out the full-color patches over my butt was 9th Infantry Division's red, white and blue cookie, the patch I wore to drill with the Washington Army National Guard two decades ago, when I was an undergrad at WSU and our Guard hadn't yet received its own squawking thunderbird insignia.

Across the top were stitched my combat patches in the "subdued desert" colors I wore them in: sand and brown. Decorating my left shoulder blade was USACAPOC with its terrible swift sword, Zeussian bolts and airborne tab; 25th

Infantry Division's "flaming pineapple" to the upper right; outboard on my right shoulder was 2nd Infantry Division's "Indian head" patch repeated. At the top center rode my Combat Action Badge, nearly obscured by rolling waves of graying hair.

It's all meaningless to most Americans, a riotous babble of colors and symbols readily forgotten if ever even momentarily grasped. To army vets, it admits of a choppy résumé, with six major unit patches to show for nine years' service. A young veteran, in line for travel pay at the VA American Lake mental health center, glanced at my back and remarked to his mother, "Looks like this guy's been everywhere."

I turned around and smiled. "Yeah.

"I have no integrity whatsoever."

Nor did I. I'd cranked out a lot of pushups during my first tour for insisting I'd be going to college when I got out. After four years of faithful service in the actives, I cut my Guard tour short in Pullman and dropped out of ROTC to hang out with my girlfriend and ride motorcycles—pretty much the same thing that happened to my junior year of high school, come to think of it.

Later a forty year-old Specialist in the Reserves, I played Falstaff to the emerging Prince Hals with dots on their collars. Redeploying, I punched out of the Reserves to go play with the 19th Group guys, then let that enlistment expire not with a bang, but a whimper.

I told them I couldn't rehabilitate my back, but it had more to do with my head and the company sergeant major knew it. That was the year I passed a Special Forces physical and was rated 70 percent disabled by the VA in the same month.

Rode into battle surrounded by heroes, but I never did anything special. Learned at the knee of sergeants who knew more then than I seem to know now, yet in five tries I'd never risen above junior NCO rank, never received a flashy medal. I kept my head down. I hauled my ruck. Always a journeyman; never a master.

Two of the insignia on my back were no longer worn by any soldiers, anywhere. Each time I shrugged on that jacket, frayed and washed out, I became a walking anachronism.

Once upon a Korean summer, I had gazed through tailor shop windows at samples of satin "tour jackets." They'd been stitching them up since the 1950s, always with the map and dragons and usually with the legend *I KNOW I'LL GO TO HEAVEN 'CAUSE I'VE SERVED MY TIME IN HELL.*

I hadn't earned it and I knew that, even if I had the forty bucks in my pocket to get one custom-embroidered. They show up in online auctions now, billed as "vintage... authentic!"

Hell? No. By the time I humped it through Korea as a private—postwar, pre-Olympics—a tour there meant Cold War anxiety, tactical discomforts, semi-lethal (i.e. you wished you had died) jungle juice and maybe the clap. Hell had been scouted, softened up and finally overrun by for-real Korean War veterans, the Forgotten Greatest Generation.

Now possessed of a humbler jacket to signify my own limited valor, I wore it everywhere, summer and winter. In weather too cold for a jeans jacket, I pulled a tin cloth work coat or a blue plaid mackinaw over it. Summers, I wore it open or slung it over my shoulder like Linus's security blanket, sometimes

with an accompanying cigar. Often with my dog at my side, or
Pretty Wife to hold my hand.

Safeguards. Defenses. Measures must be taken.

Once in awhile, I do buy a decent cigar. They taste
better than my thumb. Don't tell my doctor.

Don't tell him about the drinking, either. Two years ago,
I told the VA I don't drink anymore. It makes their
questionnaires shorter, and keeps me out of the Seattle VA
hospital basement where they hide the drunk tank out of sight.

I don't want to go there. More easily talked into things
than before, I have to watch my step to keep from being taken
care of in ways that limit life.

A service ethic does not brotherhood make. Those
embroidered flashes of angry pride separated me from always-
civilians as surely as a chauffeur's cap draws distinction from his
patron, while my long and ragged hair, bristled chin and
unpolished, slip-on shoes admitted my lapses of soldierly
discipline. Young men with stout backs and reliably lubricated
knees—men who still could carry the ball forward, hit the line
and punch through—looked away when I met their sympathetic
gazes.

Drained of utility and dispossessed of fraternity, I felt
more kinship with wizened warriors displaying the Order of
Lenin on their long, woolen greatcoats; with ghost dancers
huddled into blankets on their reservations, chanting of old
battles won only in memory; than with my fellow Americans.

Were there any?

After a while, I wore my jeans jacket less. Sometimes,
when the sun was out, I'd go out into the world armored only

jeans and a t-shirt, trying hard to remember to shift my wallet over. Every few days, I'd lose track of my jacket and have to wait for it to reappear, maybe on a jack stand under the carport or behind the truck seat or down at the coffee shop, hopefully with my wallet still in it.

This was obviously not a jacket-specific problem.

Loud booms tore enough brain tissues to affect my processing performance and RAM access. They tell me mild TBI hasn't made me an idiot, but the difference is palpable.

Would you notice if you suddenly couldn't carry a tune, or if trigonometry became a foreign language? What if you remembered what it felt like to code software transparently, but now had to do it inch by agonizing, syntactic increment? What if you couldn't pencil a measured drawing anymore? That's how the world feels to a writer who has to check definitions on the web, or defer—ever—to the shambling horror of Microsoft's grammar checker.

This is why you don't beat on your laptop with a hammer.

If I were a professional boxer, I'd have a posse to mind my stuff. Instead, I have the Veterans Administration.

They issued me a Palm Pilot sardine-packed with automated alarms and phone numbers, writing snippets and addresses and even wallet-sized photos. I learned how to scrawl computer-approved characters into it, retrieve data and jump like a hungry dog at its Pavlovian chime. Periodically, I would mislay it for a few days or simply fail to recharge it and its calendar, like my own, would reset to 2005.

"Honey, where's my jacket?"

It was raining, and Pretty Wife was waiting by the door.

"I don't know, Jack," she said. "Why don't you wear your wool coat?

"If we don't get moving, they'll be closed when we get there."

I don't get moving as readily as I used to, and almost never without gentle chivvying from my sweetie. I respect her need to do that. I acknowledge my own need to hear it. It still pisses me off, but as my ex-wife Melanie observed with adamantine constancy after I redeployed, "Everything pisses you off now."

One adapts to one's equipment. I quit poking around, grabbed a different jacket and shuffled to the car.

For five weeks, I waited for my jeans jacket to reappear before resigning myself to the fact that I'd never wear it again. Still, I quietly kept my eyes open.

That jacket was a unique piece. If it showed up on an old vet's back at the tent city where we made our monthly food donation, more power to him and I'd quietly nod in his direction. If it showed up on a college student protesting imaginary war crimes, I wasn't sure what I'd do.

"Shit or go blind" were not on the list.

On my mental operations board, I battle-updated my denim jacket's status from AWOL to MIA. Besides, we were well into the season of wool and Gore-Tex, and it was about time to quit throwing that thumb-suckin' rag over my shoulder, anyway; time to fatten up to American spec; time to get my stuff together, to quit shuffling along and glancing behind me and making cops look twice to see where I might loiter.

And it wouldn't just show up somewhere. Having fickle-fingered, fucked and forgotten me, Fate wouldn't intervene here.

Because they know the bitch, my friends didn't leave it to Fate. They pushed her aside and squared me away.

Sean, retired Marine and poet extraordinaire, scored most of the replacement patches. Tom, techno-Ranger and my old running buddy from college and the National Guard, procured the rest.

Pretty Wife, a woman long on tenacity, spends it liberally on her cranky spouse. She located what may have been the last brand-new XL Levis jacket in the Puget Sound area at South Center's Sears Roebuck, where cosseted deep amongst the pregger blouses and grime-finished, ass crack jeans of contemporary fashion they were closing out what they called "trucker's utility coats," not vintage but as authentic as any American icon made in China.

Then she broke out her sewing machine and the patches chipped in by friends, and she made it mine.

You wouldn't believe me if I told you the colors are brighter on this coat than the original, because you, un-brain damaged, remain logical enough to know that patches are just patches, uniformly the same.

Knowing and feeling are different. You probably don't believe a thin cotton jacket keeps the cold world out, either.

Shows what you know. Mine happens to be bulletproof. It's beautiful and it's the warmest garment I've ever owned.

When you see it, smile.

MORTALITY

The generation of men is like that of leaves. The wind scatters one year's leaves on the ground, but the forest burgeons and puts out others, as the season of spring comes round. So it is with men: one generation grows on, and another is passing away.

—Homer, *The Iliad*

In the end, we're fertilizer. We invent immortality so we can dream god-heroes to transport us beyond death and reassure us that we're more than that, more than meat with a punchline. We are each of us begotten in the radiant image of Adonai...

We reassure ourselves that our cultures are immortal, despite the ruins we walk over; that our philosophies and practices will resound down the epochs—and never mind the dearth of Zoroastrian evangelists chatting on Oprah.

Fertilizer we may be, but fertilizer on the hoof can always persuade itself it's something unique, something special and undoomed.

Anything but the same old shit.

Once my dad had decided he was going to fight Muhammed Ali, there was no talking him out of it.

"I'll fight him for free," he blared in his commanding tenor. "Five rounds with the champ.

"Unless he's afraid of me."

Dad wasn't entirely delusional—close, but not entirely. He knew what a fistfight was, he knew how to cover up, and he never stopped once a punch was thrown. Ali would have had to kill him.

Which he certainly would have done, in the unlikely event that the class of heavyweight boxing had assented to punching out a mid-40s businessman from Oregon. Dad probably would have let it go—another loud brag, never intended to be taken seriously—if we hadn't needled him relentlessly in the interest of his own dignity.

Ali would never lower himself, we told our father: "Rocky was a fictional character—and he was younger than you." When Dad insisted he'd fight the champ for nothing, we assured him he'd embarrass himself in the process of sustaining irreparable damage.

But Dad's a Taurus. When his lovely wife told my father he had nothing to prove, that was the red flag to his bullshit.

Muhammed Ali stood for everything Dad couldn't stand. He was a smooth hustler. He was a braggart. He played fast and loose with the rules, and he didn't know his place.

Uppity and provocative, Ali constantly yanked himself above his social station.

He was a lot like Pop in that way.

Middle age has never been the "middle" of life in the sense that what comes after will be qualitatively equivalent to what passed before. Middle age is the tipping point after which you cease becoming more yourself and begin, subtly at first, to disintegrate. Having prepared all your life to become who you are, you now get precisely one chance to do something with it—a chance that steadily recedes.

The watershed is admitting to finitude. Come up with good ways to spend your time, to enjoy and extend your personal story, and it will be called maturity, dignity, grace. Rage against time, and perhaps you'll be seen as inspired. Retreat into boy-racer dreams of bagging the prom queen, and people will point and laugh at your mid-life crisis. Perhaps you won't notice, flailing busily through the technological toy store of faux youth: treadmill, sushi maker, Porsche.

Things stop working as you remember. Coffee isn't rocket fuel anymore. More like last year's stale lawnmower gas— and that drive-through dream queen at your favorite espresso stand isn't making time. She's putting up with you, so leave a buck or two. She'll be your age soon enough.

Rubbing dirt on it won't heal you anymore, and you won't walk it off in two minutes, or even two days. Now you hurt in places you don't even remember owning, bleed for reasons you can't connect to any specific event, and it will only get worse.

Break your hand in a fight or snap your ankle climbing a rock face and you won't casually ice your grinding bones with Jack Daniels on the rocks. That's in the past. Your future advances toward cautious shuffling to avoid shattering your porcelain pelvis.

Increasingly, friends report maladies with long names that require them to be probed like alien abductees, injected, detected and slid into large machines. Everyone I know has gone from "I prolly got some aspirin around here somewhere" to pharmacopoeias bursting with the unpronounceable fruits of chemical engineering, prescribed dosage times slotted mundanely into their calendars; banal as work, meals and extracurricular enrichment for the kids.

Spend your young life as a "good healer" and the idea that you won't get better from something—ever—stings like an insult from a lower-caste universe. You just can't imagine you belong there.

Not you.

Damage is no longer temporary. Things quit healing completely. It hurts to stand, sit or breathe, but not that much really. It's frustrating when you can't pull up a word, but you'll forget the shame of it soon enough. Ever so gently—hardly even noticing—you slip from "that'll buff right out" to "*that'll* leave a mark!"

You might think disease would be a great leveler. It's certainly the popular narrative: shared distress enabling humble rediscovery of our cellular commonality. One might be forgiven for imagining that two men facing the same malady would react similarly, dispensing with politics, ego, cultural biases and fear to concentrate on the simple matter of survival.

One would, of course, be wrong.

Everyone dirges to the beat of their own drummer.

Calvin is a libertarian of long standing. If such a thing as a "dyed in the wool" Libertarian exists, Calvin is that. Calvin has also been out of corporate work for 15 months, and he's diabetic.

Problem for Calvin is that he lives in Washington, where comprehensive health plans for the self-employed are rarer than transgendered gryphons. His government-ordered COBRA health coverage is expensive, but beats hell out of no health coverage. Juxtaposing his polished loathing of government intrusion against a legitimate fear of dying untimely poses a cognitively dissonant conundrum for Cal.

Joel doesn't see it that way at all. He has no problem with the idea of public health care. It's the need for health care itself that distresses him. His medically retired, military-disabled status ensures that the Veterans Administration mails Joel's prescriptions to him auto-magically every month. Office visits to care providers are available at no charge.

Joel despises going to the doctor.

Perversely, the more broken Joel gets, the less he seeks care; the more, in fact, he resists it. Like a toddler rejecting broccoli, Joel stiff-arms prescriptions *provided at no cost*—but maybe it's not so perverse.

Joel flees the meaning of his latest battery of prescriptions, their dark gleeful whisper.

You're dyin', ol' buddy! The corpus on which your parasitic mind subsists is souring, going rank, leaving you to nibble at an increasingly malodorous, shambling simulacrum of the beautiful man your mind remembers.

Beard and hair, I grew them both out and they flowed, ruddy and unkempt, silver mixing with the blonde, alchemically transmuting cynical years to mellow reflection, hard ice squint to faded denim twinkle, bald-faced smirk to warm, crooked grin.

Turned out, my hair was naturally curly and had more body than a '64 Chrysler. Who knew? Springing out from my head in every direction, a bouncing corona of gold, silver and bronze covering a pinkish peppering of scars and a multitude of sins, it annoyed me slightly less than it amused my wife.

Along my port temple, beneath the mantle of curls, warm and crusty as fresh bread, something grew in the darkness.

Like Casey Jones, Pete Conrad mounted to the saddle, and he took his last ride to the Promised Land. Except he wasn't stoking the fires of the Cannonball Express like Casey Jones, or strapped into a tuna can with a Saturn V rocket shoved up his ass.

The retired astronaut wandered out for a gambol on his Harley-Davidson.

Pete missed a corner, shot into the pucker bushes and died where he landed. Went out the same way as T.E. Laurence—aka "Laurence of Arabia"—except that the Harley Conrad rode may actually have been a tick slower on the top end than Laurence's JAP-engined Brough Superior SS100.

But then, Laurence was a much younger man.

Commentators clucked over his bad judgment. CPT Conrad should have worn a helmet, should have watched his speed, should have taken a safety course. Most damning: he was old enough to know better. No one seems to consider that, having flown to the moon and back, he may have retained the confidence to take a big boy's chance without adult supervision.

Anyway, I'm guessing none of those precious little scolds ever worked in a nursing home.

The thing is, it's no longer anomalous, and nothing you can rage against. It's not "unfair," or "tragic," or "beyond comprehension."

The next one to go may be a surprise but won't, in the larger sense, be unexpected. Some will cheat the actuary. Others will win their bets against mutual pools of risk, bringing home a rasher of corporate bacon in one last act of defiance.

What holds us here? Works alone earn neither the grace of the moment nor the good opinion of posterity. What, then?

Charity; cats, for some; gardening, perhaps. Friends, if we're lucky: each one a strand in the cord that holds our boat to the dock, they give way gently, one by one, soundlessly unraveling our painter until we recede on the neap tide.

We each play the hand we're dealt, and some fold out of the game earlier than others. Some stand pat on the wrong hand. Others bluff away all their chips.

Timid players risk nothing, grudgingly giving up their stash one niggardly ante at a time, and it hurts to watch them and know that never—not for one tiny, shining instant—will they rare up on their two hind legs and surf that curling breaker of phony immortality. Wise prudence unwisely indulged impeaches their beauty; overmuch discretion precludes inspiration.

The graveside incantation, "In the midst of Life are we in Death," fails to note death's transitive property: that every slight brush with it enlivens our senses, knits us tighter to this slaughterhouse of our meat.

The ritual remains as backward as most of our understanding. If only for one short glimmer of fearless perfection, it is only in the midst of death that truly we are in life.

Pinklon Thomas was a surprise. Despite our teasing, we never thought Dad would actually set out on his boxing quest until he starting talking about "Jankelson's fighter."

Jankelson was a loud, fast-talking Jew of the sort who backed the choruses of my big-nosed Dad's anti-Semitic stereotypes, pitch-perfect. They were buddies and occasional business conspirators. Jankelson managed a young boxer who was moving his way up the ranks.

"Jankelson has a heavyweight who needs experience," Dad said. "I'm gonna go five rounds with him."

We drove north to scout Thomas's fight in Seattle, and sat in the front row. It was the first bout I'd ever attended. From the front row of folding chairs, I could see every stitch in their shoes. It felt wrong to sit there in that moist, loud, sinful room where people got paid for what Mom said not to do.

We left with spit and blood in our hair, less from the heavyweight class than from a vicious flyweight bout. A Puerto Rican lost that decision to a redheaded Irishman with a sweet smile and a wicked left, but the putative winner seeped blood from every freckle.

Thomas, a fighter on his way up, gently whupped meatball Roger Braxton by technical knockout. Braxton was a strong puncher but Thomas moved around the ring like a cat, probing and flowing, watching his opponent the way black men in the bus station watched cops out of the corners of their eyes. My big sister promptly conceived an exotic crush but Dad, who never duked it in a sanctioned fight that I know of, was roundly unimpressed.

"Thomas hasn't got any chest. No chest!" Dad, just getting underway, blared on. "His punches are wispy. He slaps and pats like a little girl."

Jill rolled her eyes as Dad rambled on.

"Jankelson thinks he's got a glass jaw. I'll knock him out in the third round."

It never happened. Five years later, Dad was administering a retirement community, Muhammed Ali was battling Parkinson's, and Pinklon Thomas was the heavyweight champion of the world.

"I'm back," I told her, striding through our front door with my old accustomed military flattop over a still-full beard.

"Wow," said Pretty Wife. "You look... younger."

Friends told me the same thing when my hair got long, almost ubiquitously with the blessed exception of one senior lesbian activist who winked and hugged me and spat into my ear, "You *dirty hippie!*"

We all know we're getting older. We've seen our own baby pictures. We've obligatorily admired wedding pictures of the firm, lovely people who shrunk into our wrinkly grands. But after a certain point, no one ever tells you—under any conditions whatsoever—that you look older. It is considered bad juju, and worse form.

At the rate I'm lately reported to be youthing, I'm practically neo-natal by now. Well-prepared, anyway, for my second childhood.

Pretty Wife asked "Are you going to shave, too?"

"Sure," I said and headed for the bathroom, idly scratching at my left temple.

I've lived long enough to watch the rise of marvels: space stations and Teletubbies, American Idol's instantaneous electoral validation, un-siamesing of the conjoined, the technometaphysics of virtual worship and even serious people striving earnestly to define transnational terrorism as distinct from multinational corporatism. But who, in their most lurid, *Future Shock*-inspired, dystopic mind jag could have predicted an elective procedure of surgically installed flatulence?

"Don't worry," came the technician's reassuring voice as she jammed an ostrich leg backward up my scrubbed and shining gut, "it won't smell at all."

I didn't answer her, electing to simply lie there whimpering, hugging my knees to my chest, panting fitfully like a virgin mother laboring in reverse and praying to any available sympathetic deity that a video of this wasn't being prepared for some Internet dungeon site.

The time has come to put away childish things, and pick up the terrifying implements of modern medicine. For the first time since belated adolescence, rites of passage proliferate around me like bouncing, bleeping antagonists of Super Mario Brothers.

Prime time on premium cable is over, leaving me to sit through all those commercials I thought I'd skipped, in between low-def reruns of "I Love Lucy" and "Gilligan's Island" delivered off-air via badly adjusted rabbit ears.

Settling my decreasingly comfortable frame into the worn cushions of my life, I poke dyspeptically at the buttons of a remote control bolted to a swivel on a nightstand layered in a peeling veneer of richly grained Melamine, but the channel won't change. Onscreen, I get no *Bonanza* of big-hatted heroes, no immortal stud Captain Kirk sidling up on impulse power to face down the ghetto Klingons.

No. There is only one channel, narrowcasting endless reruns of the heaving tissuescape of my gurgling pink colon, curving on to forever.

Everyone gets it in the end.

Calvin posts a web cam shot, sending his image—one of hundreds, perhaps thousands—splashing out into a meta-networked maelstrom of clashingly disjunctive paradigms that has grown more complex than governments can regulate or corporations tether to board-certified, bottom-line results.

As have all gods, our latest construct assures us of grace, eternality of mind and its own invincible primacy. In a novel twist, this deity actually is both demonstrably tangible <u>and</u> unimaginably complex.

An early acolyte, Calvin ascended to the priesthood and for some years has humbly served as *de facto* apostle, transcending evangelism both by faith and by works.

Countenance unchanged, he slumps in a dim room, baptized in the gentle luminescence of a flat screen monitor, slack and massive arms acolytically prepared, spectacles reflecting the constant parturition of ideas rushing from countless many sires and dams to join the deathless, adoring, worshipful rabble of congregation—or is it Legion?

Over the years of his web presence, only one change has rippled over the beatific solemnity of St. Calvin, and I regret to say it's not a fresh t-shirt. His latest web cam images include, cradled carefully in his non-mousing arm, an infant grandchild.

Relegated to a desktop background in support of the pink chubbiness of this new piece of wetware, Cal appears newly ancient, pale, dissolute, wraithlike.

Immortal.

A month ago, I went to bury another friend. How "good" a friend was he? You tell me. I don't grade my friends on a curve.

Christian was a car guy, unlike his dad Noel who is a former employer of mine. Noel and I aren't car guys.

We ride bikes. Triumphs, Guzzis, BMWs, the odd Honda for leavening—our Eurasian mistresses don't keep us young, but they whisper vital lies, moaning and straining beneath us as we hold them down to the road.

Noel and I kid ourselves that we're fast, but if we're all racing the same road, it's hard to avoid concluding that Christian beat us both. A friggin' car guy. That's how it goes, I guess.

A few years ago, I sold my bellowing red Ducati 900 Super Sport to Christian's father. Like Christian himself, it was cranky, temperamental, deeply flawed—and a joy and pleasure on its game. Then there were the other times. It went through ignition coils like an Amsterdam exchange goes through needles.

One day, a year or three after I didn't work for his dad anymore, I walked into the store from the front lot where I had noticed the company truck, to which I also felt a bit of a connection. It was a bright new Chevy 1500 W/T that had replaced the battered '68 Jimmy called "Old Blue."

Noel's father's father, founder of the family store, originally bought Blue. When I worked there I had started a small sub-franchise for Noel, and it eventually paid for a new company truck for the store. This pleased me.

Now the entire right side was stove in, stem to stern. Christian was the first guy I saw when I came through the door, so I joked him a little.

"Chris, d'jou already crash th' new truck?"

"I don't wanna fuckin' talk about it," Christian said, stomping back to his inventory desk near the loading dock.

Wicked hangover this morning, the kind you beg G-D to take from you and promise anything—any sacrifice, be it goat, son or birthright—in cheap barter for a moment's relief, or at least for the mess of pottage stirred from caffeine, ibuprofen, sugar, acetaminophen, sweetened lard and pseudo-epinephrine. But there's no alcohol in my system; no oxy, ex or meth.

Nothing so dull receding from my central nervous system, crisping lobes of liver on its way out the back.

Yesterday the new motorcycle, thunderous and demon black, took me up the mountain, closer to G-D, backward through time, skittering to the crumbling edge of a highway falling into the dark side of forever.

The road to Paradise is crowded and over-patrolled, but there is another road, on another mountain. Strait and narrow, heaved and broken, often closed: you can go that way with friends, but you'll reach the end alone. Giggling, if your moment of grace is unexpired; steaming and bleeding in the other event.

Promise broken, then.

Pretty Wife and I traded pledges to stay away from stupid before she embarked for the Holy Land of Perennial Combat and I settled in to hold down our little suburban fort. Saddling up with the mousiest of good intentions, I waddled down Maple Valley Highway toward our Black Diamond link-up at a respectable, middle-aged pace. Wincing at the pain shooting up from the low bars into my wrists, and fairly nauseated by the effect of high footpegs on the squashed intervertebral disks in my low back and neck, I reminded myself to dispense with sportbikes and settle on a more mature form of juvenile self-expression. Internet porn, maybe.

The way to Windy Ridge goes winding up the backside of Mount St. Helens, steaming sullenly ever since her brush with fame after publicly blowing her top.

The very Brittney Spears of northwest peaks, St. Helens inveigles a constant stream of suitors to mount her fecund flanks even as she plots her next sticky hot eruption, mumbling stuporously to herself about what happened to her smooth figure and why sensible people keep their distance.

There are no suburban green street signs there, only yellow warning diamonds imploring your prudence. Pavement along that route is cracked and broken, frost-heaved and potholed.

The worst insults to surface integrity are outlined in fluorescent pink traffic paint. At 80 mph in a corner marked for 20, the pink squiggles induce target fixation the way Coleman lanterns invite moths to a neighborly barbeque.

Masquerading as our own youth, if only for the bracing dose of stupidity that's in it, we broke the law for hours, each according to his personal gospel of survivability and the degree to which he'd been anointed with the fragrant oils of adrenaline. For the first time in too long—first time since my last promise, anyway—I leaned far enough over to conjure demons out of the ground and leave them standing flat-footed, staring after me and holding the bag of my mortal aches and pains and limiting fears, forgotten. Somewhere on that road lies a broken left peg feeler, looking for all the world like an edge-ground, black-anodized bone pin.

When services let out, I was tired, sweaty, sore—and 150 miles from home.

Joel shoots up regularly now. It's treating him right. Drug vials and mil-spec Skilcraft needles show up in his mailbox, regular as teenaged masturbation, and self-injection has transformed from a fear to a comforting ritual for Joel.

He used to explain to me that you can't let up for an instant, can't let the bastards grind you down, can't let your guard down, gotta keep your shit tight and whatever you do, don't blink.

"Man, I don't know why it took me so long to try this," Joel says now. "I feel *great!*"

"Dude, you *look* great," I assure him, and it's even true. Joel's lost part of his paunch-pack since he went on the needle, and his color flushed back into human range. If I squint it even looks like he's re-growing some hair, but that's probably the group hallucination brought on by mutual enthusiasm.

Changing up his drug of choice was a wise move. Insulin is working much better for Joel than booze did. He's addicted to it the way Pretty Wife is to birth control and I am to analgesics: really just not himself without it. I'd toast his progress, but alcohol's off-limits now. No more howling at the moon from a Pullman lanai while we drain off mason jars of gin.

"For real, Joel, you look ten years younger."

Whinging once about the increasing unreadiness of my crumbling carcass to handle "what might come up," I received summary benediction from my dauntless VA counselor.

"You can do whatever you need to do," Björn reminded me. "You just gotta understand you're gonna pay for it."

Sure and the piper came this morning, blaring bagpipe solos of burning knees, percussively crunching joints and the soaring arpeggios of tendinitis. Against my better judgment and my word, I spent some of my principal capital riding that mountain road. One dancing sunbeam leading me into triple-digit silviculture and I might have blown the whole wad.

Can that ever be worth it?

There's no financial payoff for a fast ride with friends, and no glory whatever in sacrificing your prized motorcycle on a cliffstone oubliette. Are you stupid enough to bet your life against that fleeting, fragrant whiff of immortality? Is it that important not to blink? If you believe you even have a choice, you probably do. Take a step back from the edge, ride home at the pace of sensible men, and kiss your family.

Sometimes I don't. The devil stands behind me wearing toe cleavage pumps and designer décolletage. She strokes my hair while I bet, laughing at pot limits.

Sometimes I have to push in the whole stack. On the day that I lose, she'll laugh again and raise an eyebrow at the Dealer.

Maybe she'll tip me a wink as they escort me out the back.

The bow of my glasses finally fouled on it enough times for me to notice. I poked at it, laying a finger alongside my temple like some underdressed Ben Franklin analogue. I felt something warm and furry, like a tiny rodent battened to my skull.

"Honey, could you look at something for me?"

The VA nurse line operator ran down her standardized checklist to affirm that I had a dermal lesion, irregular, approximately a centimeter across, recently grown, slightly crusty.

"Sir, have you been in the sun?"

"You mean like when I was out gardening yesterday, or like when I deployed to Iraq?"

"So you have, or haven't, been in the sun?"

Google is not my friend. Think you'd like to know more about cancer and, y'know, kinda be *empowered* that way?

You're wrong.

My dad is 79 years old now. He's broken his back twice, lost a pair of multi-million dollar fortunes. He's on his fifth marriage, has his name on a university building. He's working out a bankruptcy.

Dad drives a bus to supplement his Air Force retirement stipend, and recently fell out the back door helping kids down during an emergency drill. He doesn't want to jump into the squared circle anymore, but Dad gives ground only grudgingly: he still asserts that he'll live to 124.

Ali, already one of the most recognized men on the planet, went on to become one of the most beloved elder statesmen of sports. Of Muhammed Ali these days, Dad says only, "He seems like a good man."

Of the passage of a son before his parents, the funereal priest intoned, "There are no words."

Of course there were words, but they were ugly words: addiction, overdose, vomit, asphyxia. Yesterday, when the sun revealed itself in eye-lancing brilliance over winter snow, it felt at last far enough removed from strained words at a funeral reception line for me to drive down to the store and talk to Noel. I invited him on a motorcycle ride, because that's all I know how to say that makes the least lick of sense.

"Yeah, I might do that," Noel said. "Only put about a hundred miles on the Triumph all last year.

"I've been driving the truck to work. You know, I had a lot of stuff with Christian to deal with, driving him down to AA and all..."

I have a startling number of risk-tolerant friends with odd habits. Some of them die ugly. That's the way of things, too. If they knew ahead of time that they would die ugly, would they have changed the oddity of their habits just for that? Maybe not. Probably not.

I hope not.

We chatted about the usual crap. Boys, college, girls, jobs, music, family, books: these form the backdrop to the stage on which we dance from time to time, all too rarely together. When the twins were born I wrote, in a spasm of callow melodrama, *they are their father's executioners.*

If only.

We buried her twin in a short white casket, leaving Daughtergirl my only tenuous thread to posterity. Unlike losing a friend in middle age, Flavia's death *was* unfair. It *was* tragic.

It was so far beyond comprehension as to cause me to tear out every god cowering in my soul by their clinging roots and attempt the murder of them all. I couldn't kill them, as it turned out; couldn't even make them bleed. They were gods, after all.

Because no mere man's rage is powerful enough to dethrone immortals, I locked them away from my view. Years later, stumbling across the dusty cupboard where I'd imprisoned my gods, I peered in disinterestedly.

Nothing was there.

I grew a new mole, was all. A big, hairy rascal parked just where the old one was excised and biopsied years ago. The VA dermatology resident hosed down the side of my head with a spray can of cryogenic fluid and razored it away, resulting in no more pain than a brutal Slurpee brain freeze.

No worries, then. I knew all along it was probably nothing.

"Actually, it's this I want to get a better look at," said the attending physician, laying a cool, purple-vinyled finger onto my face. Her large hazel eyes, framed by café-apropos spectacles, focused intently on my face. Touching her fingertip gently, I felt a small white dot high up alongside the bridge of my nose.

"Oh, I've had that for years."

Looking portentously over her glasses at her junior, she spoke with authority.

"Biopsy it."

The young VA resident, compliant flesh mechanic, pulled a needle off the tray. He charged it with Novocain. He raised its gleaming tip slowly toward my right eye.

I blinked.

ABOUT THE AUTHOR

Since he won't be well-known until he's dead, Jack Lewis advises that you buy a lovely first edition of this book right now and promises to autograph it when you catch him.

Jack owns two motorcycles and a chainsaw, drinks Ardbeg if you're buying and prefers slip-on shoes. Having turned his hand variously to furniture repair, telecommunications, soldiering and sheep farming, he hopes to make a living at writing. Jack's work appears regularly in anthologies and periodicals and on his website, www.jaxworx.com.

He lives north of Seattle in a small house with a small family and a very large dog. *Nothing In Reserve* is his second book.

THANKS AND APPRECIATION

For editorial feedback, encouragement and butt-kickings:
Andrew Carroll, Kathleen Cain and HMarc Lewis.

For quality assurance, Litsam thanks our Beta Readers.

First, most egregious, and largest number of errors:
Carl Paukstis (7)

In order of initial report:
Glenn Stone (2)
Dennis Weatherly (1)
Philip Kopp (3)
Andrew Kinman (2)
Dean Woodward (endnotes)

To become a Beta Reader yourself, please visit www.litsam.com.

Several superlative people are owed our particular thanks.

For permission to use lyrics from *Things That I Have Seen*: Mr. Richard Shindell.

For permission to use lyrics from *Coal Town Road* © Cabot Trail Music (SOCAN): Mr. Allister MacGillivray.

For attempting to allow use of lyrics from *Superman*: Mr. John Ondrasik.

Shasta Willson for photography, layout and book design.
Wikimedia and Riverwood124 for cover image of sniper.
Wikimedia and Geographicus Rare Antique Maps for map.

For making life worth living: my girls.

Made in the USA
Charleston, SC
11 May 2011